Software Reviews and Audits Handbook

WILEY SERIES IN
SOFTWARE ENGINEERING PRACTICE

SERIES EDITORS:
Patrick A.V. Hall, Brunel University, UK
Martyn A. Ould, Praxis Systems plc, UK
William E. Riddle, Software Design & Analysis, Inc., USA

Fletcher J. Buckley • Implementing Software Engineering Practices
John J. Marciniak and Donald J. Reifer • Software Acquisition Management
John S. Hares • SSADM for the Advanced Practitioner
Martyn A. Ould • Strategies for Software Engineering: The Management of Risk and Quality
David P. Youll • Making Software Development Visible: Effective Project Control
Charles P. Hollocker • Software Reviews and Audits Handbook

Software Reviews and Audits Handbook

CHARLES P. HOLLOCKER

A Wiley-Interscience Publication
John Wiley & Sons, Inc.
New York / Chichester / Brisbane / Toronto / Singapore

*To Raymond Charles and Paul Joseph who,
together with my wife, Cindy, provided
ample motivation, support and interlude.*

In recognition of the importance of preserving what has been written, it is a policy of John Wiley & Sons, Inc. to have books of enduring value published in the United States printed on acid-free paper, and we exert our best efforts to that end.

Copyright © 1990 by John Wiley & Sons, Inc.

All rights reserved. Published simultaneously in Canada.

Reproduction or translation of any part of this work beyond that permitted by Section 107 or 108 of the 1976 United States Copyright Act without the permission of the copyright owner is unlawful. Requests for permission or further information should be addressed to the Permissions Department, John Wiley & Sons, Inc.

Library of Congress Cataloging in Publication Data:
Hollocker, Charles P.
    Software reviews and audits handbook / Charles P. Hollocker.

     p. cm.–(Wiley series in software engineering practice)
    Includes bibliographical references and index.
    1. Computer software–Validation. 2. Computer software--Verification. I. Title. II. Series.

QA76.76.V47H65   1990
005.1'4–dc20   90-12432
ISBN 0-471-51401-2   CIP

Printed in the United States of America

10 9 8 7 6 5 4 3 2 1

CONTENTS

List of Figures   xiii

Preface   xv

1 Introduction   1

    1.1 Purpose, 2
    1.2 Audience, 2
    1.3 The Approach Taken, 2
    1.4 The Language Used, 2
    1.5 A Handbook Overview, 4

2 Program Framework   6

    2.1 Product Realization, 7
        2.1.1 Process Definition, 8
        2.1.2 Process Control, 9
        2.1.3 Process Environment, 12
    2.2 Process Improvement, 13
        2.2.1 Controlling Improvement, 15
        2.2.2 Supporting Improvement, 17
    2.3 Review & Audit Taxonomy, 17
        2.3.1 Project Reviews, 19
        2.3.2 Product Reviews, 20
        2.3.3 Audits, 22

2.4 Summary, 23

3 Project Reviews 24

3.1 Management Review Process, 24
    3.1.1 Objective, 24
    3.1.2 People and Their Agendas, 25
    3.1.3 When to Hold a Management Review, 25
    3.1.4 Procedures, 25
    3.1.5 Output, 26
3.2 Specific Process Applications, 26
    3.2.1 Project Reviews for Product Realization, 26
        3.2.1.1 Concept Closure, 27
        3.2.1.2 Project Definition, 27
        3.2.1.3 Product Realization, 28
        3.2.1.4 Trial Readiness, 28
        3.2.1.5 General Market Availability, 29
        3.2.1.6 Product Maturity Review, 29
        3.2.1.7 Product Retirement Review, 29
    3.2.2 Project Reviews for Process Improvement, 30
        3.2.2.1 Project Sponsorship, 30
        3.2.2.2 Cause Definition, 31
        3.2.2.3 Remedy Identification & Trial Readiness, 31
        3.2.2.4 Remedy Proven, 32
        3.2.2.5 Remedy Transitioned, 32
3.3 The Implementation Challenge, 32
    3.3.1 Acceptance and Participation, 33
        3.3.1.1 Unique Product Realization Issues, 33
        3.3.1.2 Unique Process Improvement Issues, 34
    3.3.2 Execution Consistency, 35
        3.3.2.1 Unique Product Realization Issues, 36
        3.3.2.2 Unique Process Improvement Issues, 36
    3.3.3 Feedback, 37
        3.3.3.1 Unique Product Realization Issues, 37
        3.3.3.2 Unique Process Improvement Issues, 38
3.4 Summary, 39

4 Product Reviews 41

4.1 The Technical Review, 41
    4.1.1 Objective, 41

- 4.1.2 People and Their Agendas, 42
- 4.1.3 When to Hold A Technical Review Meeting, 42
- 4.1.4 Procedures, 43
  - 4.1.4.1 Planning, 43
  - 4.1.4.2 Overview, 43
  - 4.1.4.3 Preparation, 43
  - 4.1.4.4 Examination, 43
- 4.1.5 Output, 44

4.2 The Software Inspection, 44
- 4.2.1 Objective, 44
- 4.2.2 People and Their Agendas, 45
- 4.2.3 When to Hold the Inspection Meeting, 46
- 4.2.4 Procedures, 46
  - 4.2.4.1 Planning, 46
  - 4.2.4.2 Overview, 47
  - 4.2.4.3 Preparation, 47
  - 4.2.4.4 Examination, 47
- 4.2.5 Output, 48

4.3 The Walkthrough, 48
- 4.3.1 Objective, 48
- 4.3.2 People and Their Agendas, 49
- 4.3.3 When to Hold the Walkthrough Meeting, 49
- 4.3.4 Procedures, 49
  - 4.3.4.1 Planning, 49
  - 4.3.4.2 Overview, 50
  - 4.3.4.3 Preparation, 50
  - 4.3.4.4 Examination, 50
- 4.3.5 Output, 50

4.4 Implementation Challenge, 50
- 4.4.1 Application Opportunities, 51
  - 4.4.1.1 Software Planning, 51
  - 4.4.1.2 Software Products, 51
- 4.4.2 Process Mix Planning, 52
  - 4.4.2.1 Considerations, 52
  - 4.4.2.2 Review Process Comparison, 53
  - 4.4.2.3 The Verification and Validation Plan, 55
- 4.4.3 Multiple Examinations, 56
  - 4.4.3.1 Motivation, 56
  - 4.4.3.2 Walkthrough of Requirements, 56

            4.4.3.3   The Technical Review of Requirements, 57
            4.4.3.4   The Inspection of the Specification, 57
    4.4.4   Acceptance and Participation, 58
    4.4.5   Execution Consistency, 59
    4.4.6   Feedback, 61
  4.5   Summary, 64

5 Audits   65

  5.1   The Audit Process, 65
    5.1.1   Objective, 65
    5.1.2   People and Their Agendas, 66
    5.1.3   When To Audit, 66
    5.1.4   Procedures, 66
    5.1.5   Output, 69
  5.2   Specific Process Applications, 69
    5.2.1   The Software Quality Program Audit, 69
    5.2.2   The In-process Audit, 71
            5.2.2.1   Example Product Consistency Audit, 71
            5.2.2.2   Example Audit of Process Execution, 72
    5.2.3   Configuration Audits, 72
            5.2.3.1   The Physical Configuration Audit, 73
            5.2.3.2   The Functional Configuration Audit, 74
  5.3   Implementation Challenge, 75
    5.3.1   The Challenge of Auditing, 75
    5.3.2   Audit Leadership, 77
    5.3.3   The Auditor, 78
    5.3.4   The Seven Sins, 79
  5.4   Summary, 79

6 Special Topics   82

  6.1   Interviewing, 82
    6.1.1   Preparation, 82
    6.1.2   Elements of Success, 82
    6.1.3   Skill Improvement, 83
    6.1.4   Active Listening, 83
    6.1.5   Questioning, 83
  6.2   Report Writing, 84
    6.2.1   Audit Plans, 84
    6.2.2   Results Report, 85

      6.2.3   Recommendations Report, 85
      6.2.4   Executive Summary, 87
      6.2.5   Literary Suicide, 87
  6.3   Role of Quality Management, 88

7 A Guess and A Vision   92

  7.1   The Vision and The Journey, 93
  7.2   Program Overview, 93
  7.3   Knowledge Base Maintenance, 94
  7.4   Award and Reward, 94
  7.5   Decision Support, 95
  7.6   Recommendations, 96

Appendix 1: Checklists   98

Program Checklists   101

Process Definition, 101
Process Controls, 103
Quality Management, 104
Configuration Management, 106
Project Management, 108
Process Environment, 110
Information Management, 111
Program Evolution, 113

Project Checklists for Product Realization   115

Executive Project Evaluation, 115
Concept Closure: Preparation Areas, 117
    Concept Closure: The Product, 117
    Concept Closure: The Process, 117
    Concept Closure: The Project, 118
    Concept Closure: (Business) Environment, 118
Project Definition: Preparation Areas, 119
    Project Definition: The Product, 119
    Project Definition: The Process, 120
    Project Definition: The Project, 121
    Project Definition: (Business) Environment, 122
Product Realization: Preparation Areas, 123
    Product Realization: The Product, 123

Product Realization: The Process, 124
Product Realization: The Project, 124
Product Realization: (Business) Environment, 124
Trial Readiness: Preparation Areas, 125
Trial Readiness: The Product, 126
Trial Readiness: The Process, 127
Trial Readiness: The Project, 128
Trial Readiness: (Business) Environment, 129
General Market Availability: Preparation Areas, 130
General Market Availability: The Product, 130
General Market Availability: The Process, 131
General Market Availability: The Project, 132
General Market Availability: (Business) Environment, 132
Product Maturity: Preparation Areas, 133
Product Maturity: The Product, 134
Product Maturity: The Process, 134
Product Maturity: The Project, 135
Product Maturity: (Business) Environment, 135
Product Retirement: Preparation Areas, 136
Product Retirement: The Product, 137
Product Retirement: The Process, 137
Product Retirement: The Project, 138
Product Retirement: (Business) Environment, 138

Project Checklists for Process Improvement   139

Executive Project Evaluation, 139
PIP Project Sponsorship: Preparation Areas, 140
PIP Project Sponsorship: The Team, 140
PIP Project Sponsorship: The Improvement, 141
PIP Project Sponsorship: The Work, 142
PIP Cause Definition: Preparation Areas, 143
PIP Cause Definition: The Team, 143
PIP Cause Definition: The Improvement, 144
PIP Cause Definition: The Work, 144
PIP Remedy ID and Trial Ready: Preparation Areas, 145
PIP Remedy ID and Trial Ready: The Team, 145
PIP Remedy ID and Trial Ready: The Improvement, 146
PIP Remedy ID and Trial Ready: The Work, 146

CONTENTS **xi**

    PIP Remedy Proven: Preparation Areas, 147
        PIP Remedy Proven: The Team, 147
        PIP Remedy Proven: The Improvement, 148
        PIP Remedy Proven: The Work, 148
    PIP Remedy Transitioned: Preparation Areas, 149
        PIP Remedy Transitioned: The Team, 150
        PIP Remedy Transitioned: The Improvement, 150
        PIP Remedy Transitioned: The Work, 151

Process Checklists   153

    Common Process Concerns, 153
    Product Review Implementation, 154
    Project Review Implementation, 155
    Audit Implementation, 156

Product Checklists   157

    General Document Requirements, 157
    Requirements Documentation, 158
    Common Design Document Issues, 159
    Architectural Design Document, 160
    Detailed Design Documentation, 161
    Code, 162
    Common Test Plan Issues, 163
    Test Specifications, 165
    Test Reports and Records, 166

Appendix 2:   Sample Forms   167

Audit Forms   168

    Interview Worksheet, 168
    Interview Feedback, 169

Project Review Forms   170

    Project Milestone Declaration, 170
    Product Release Authorization, 171
    Improvement Project Authorization Request, 172
    Improvement Project Progress Record, 173

Inspection Forms — 174

Inspection Meeting Notice, 174
Discussion Items List, 175
Inspection Report Form, 177

Appendix 3: Sample Letters — 178

Software Quality Program Audit (SQPA) Announcement, 179
SQPA Preparation, 180
Review of Audit Results, 184
Delivery of Audit Results, 185
Post-Audit Recommendations, 186

Appendix 4: Plans and Reports — 187

Audit Plans and Reports — 188

Software Quality Program Audit (SQPA) Audit Plan,, 188
SQPA Results Report, 196
SQPA Recommendations Report, 209
SQPA Executive Summary, 215
Test Verification Report, 220

Inspection Plans and Reports — 226

Weekly Inspection Report, 226
Monthly Inspection Summary, 228

Appendix 5: References — 230

IEEE Standards — 230

Department of Defense Standards — 231

Books — 231

Articles — 232

Index — 237

LIST OF FIGURES

2-1 Process Controls, 10

2-2 Control Conflicts, 11

2-3 The "Quality Cost" Family of Curves, 13

2-4 Apparent Curve Inversion, 14

2-5 Software Error Costs Increase Throughout the Lifecycle, 14

2-6 Cost and Revenue as Related to the Framework, 15

2-7 Some Distinctions: Reviews versus Audits, 18

2-8 Boehm's Dis-Economies of Scale, 21

3-1 The Sinking Ship, 34

4-1 Product Abstraction versus Time, 53

4-2 Process Distinctions for Product Reviews, 54

4-3 Ensuring Review Program Acceptance, 59

4-4 Sample Required Reviewer Matrix, 60

4-5 Before the Review, 62

4-6 During the Review, 62

4-7 After the Review, 62

5-1 The Seven Sins, 80

6-1 SQPA Results Report Outline, 86

6-2 SQPA Recommendations Report Outline, 86
6-3 SQPA Executive Summary Outline, 88
6-4 Characterizing the Quality Function, 89
6-5 Sample Activities within the Quality Function Taxonomy, 89
6-6 Typical Quality Management Involvement with Reviews and Audits, 90
6-7 A Standards Taxonomy, 91
7-1 Achieving the Vision, 94
7-2 Economies of Timing, 95
7-3 Measurement Opportunities, 96

PREFACE

The responsibility for quality rests with every member of the working community, but it begins at the top with executive commitment. If affordable excellence is our goal, then motivation for applying software reviews and audits is compelling. Here are two observations:

1. Reviews have proven themselves the most cost-effective mechanism for improving quality.
2. Failure to verify as true that which you believe to be true allows risks to become unmanageable.

The first satisfies our customers and keeps us in business. The second does not satisfy them and may put us out of business. Audits can help avoid that situation.

Project reviews provide the foundation for focusing the company as a team to succeed. By managing explicitly for schedule, cost, and quality, we tell each organizational element and worker on a project what is needed to provide products that are truly fit for use. Exchanges including goals, constraints, and assumptions allow us to manage trade-offs and high risks *before* they disrupt the project's chances for success. A forum for assessing progress and reaffirming direction, the project review represents one of the first steps that can be taken to run the project like a business.

With regard to product reviews, this handbook represents a challenge to everyone participating in software development. Know your immediate customers, understand their requirements, and provide them a forum to participate and provide you with valuable product improvement feedback. Work together with them for continuous improvement of that forum. The standard process descriptions for technical reviews, inspections, and walkthroughs offered in this *Handbook* provide you with a sound starting point to improve communications, the quality of delivered products, and the sense of participation and achievement.

Without audits, our customers may know our most severe problems before we do. Quality program coverage, both in intent and execution, are best determined within the company. Audits are an important element of controlling change. Whether focusing on our products or our processes, audits confirm conformance to standards and this goes a long way toward ensuring consistency between products and documented baselines, and consistency in the application and execution of our processes.

This *Handbook* is intended to supplement knowledge within your company by providing process definitions and materials valuable to the implementation of your own program of reviews and audits. The materials found in the appendixes are representative of those found in successful programs. However, because the *Handbook* addresses many issues, these materials are intended for general reference. You are encouraged to use the *Handbook* as a resource to create materials specific to your needs.

CHARLES P. HOLLOCKER

Richardson, Texas

CHAPTER 1

Introduction

Admittedly, reviews and audits have gained the increased attention of software engineering management during the 1980s. However, the extensive research efforts of government, industry, and academia have produced no single methodology to combat the unwanted trademarks of software development. Projects tend to be late and over budget, if even completed, and produce products whose quality is largely unpredictable. Certainly, then, the reasonable approach is to apply those industry-proven methodologies and techniques that offer the greatest return on your investment. But what are they? And even more important, how do they fit together? Unless your *process* research budget is uncommonly substantial, your company probably labels these questions as too philosophic. Pragmatically, then, where can you start?

Regardless of your selection and blend of available technologies, reviews and audits can play an integral part in making your development program a successful one. Across the industry, the use of reviews and audits has shown a substantial return on investment. Traditional testing is too capital-intensive and begins too late in the development process to provide the magnitude of cost savings that can be realized by the application of reviews and audits. By increasing our investment in early defect detection and avoidance through the application of reviews and audits, we can often reduce the cost of software quality [Hollocker, 1986] by up to 30 percent.

With myriad approaches stated in the literature and present in our companies, it remains difficult to discern just what a "review" or "audit" really is and how they might be best used. This difficulty increases when we hear the terms *inspection* and *walkthrough*. Good definitions should include a general description that identifies a set as well as information isolating the item being defined from other members of the set. This approach has been taken here.

1.1 PURPOSE

This handbook has been designed to empower its readers with specific *process definitions*, guidance on *when to use* them, and sample (editable) materials assisting the reader with *how to use* them. Given the "what, when, and how" of reviews and audits, the reader is well equipped to establish or improve a formal program of reviews and audits. The result should be seen in an improved ability to meet delivery schedules within budget and a flexibility that promotes continuous improvement. Reviews and audits are instrumental in providing product and process quality.

1.2 AUDIENCE

This handbook is particularly aimed at those individuals who are responsible for the software quality program. Others who will benefit from reading the handbook include the multitude of people responsible for requiring, scheduling, or performing specific reviews or audits. Their reading of the text, although more selective, will be aided by the approach taken in developing the handbook.

1.3 THE APPROACH TAKEN

Based on the belief that most people are better editors than writers, this handbook helps prevent the time-consuming and expensive rediscovery of the fundamentals of reviews and audits. It does so by providing individuals responsible for the software quality program with a primary source of reference rich with materials that are easily tailored to specific needs. Readers may have responsibilities spanning three levels of control abstraction: (1) control of the overall program, (2) project controls, and (3) control of individual processes and resulting products. This handbook has been structured for these readers and the treatment is both definitive and pragmatic.

1.4 THE LANGUAGE USED

One important organizational factor of this book (and present as a recurring theme throughout) is that distinctions are made among process, project, program, and product.

A *process* is viewed as a set of steps that organize work and result in an initial or improved work product. The process best facilitates control when it is consistently applied and its results are both observable and repeatable. Process documentation, whether descriptive or prescriptive, is valuable toward achieving these goals and is a necessary audit benchmark.

One iteration of process application, then, is a *project*. This level of control is where business concerns are brought into consideration along with the technology issues of process execution.

A *program* is the next level of abstraction up from the project. The business entity responsible for one or more consecutive or concurrent projects must have a program for ensuring the company's success.

Processes executed as part of a project produce the *product*(s). In the discussion of product reviews, the term *software element* will be used. The *IEEE Standard for Software Reviews and Audits* [IEEE, 1028] defines a software element as:

> A deliverable or in-process document produced or acquired during software development or maintenance. Specific examples include but are not limited to:
>
> 1. Project planning documents (for example, software development plans, and software verification and validation plans)
> 2. Software requirements and design specifications
> 3. Test effort documentation (i.e., as described in ANSI/IEEE Std 829-1983)
> 4. Customer-deliverable documentation
> 5. Program source code
> 6. Representation of software solutions implemented in firmware
> 7. Reports (for example, review, audit, project status) and data (for example, defect detection, test)

Verification is determining whether or not the products of a given step of software development fulfill the requirements established during the previous step. *Validation*, on the other hand, looks back not one step but all the way back to requirements to evaluate software at the end of development to ensure compliance with software requirements. Together, verification and validation activities provide evidence that a sequential and auditable (traceable) process has been used to develop the software, which leads us to product technology and process technology.

Product technology is used to describe the level of functionality, performance, or other characteristics possessed by a particular product or family of products. It is most definitely tied to the "newness" of the need for the product, or anticipated success at culturing some new need. The newer "open" computer architectures and the quest for standard interfaces are two product technology issues that are becoming increasingly familiar. Providing a new processor chip that would fit on the head of a pin would certainly be a product technology breakthrough. *Process technology*, by comparison, is less visible to the public and is often of lesser status if recognized by the company. Process technology is used to describe the effectiveness, efficiency, or other characteristics of how we work. Productivity, for example, is a process technology issue.

Catching problems as early as possible is the emphasis of reviews and audits. Whether the defects are in the specification of requirements, in the design, in the code, or in the way we go about the business of software development, earlier identification and removal means dollars saved.

The preceding definitions, although rather brief, are critically important from a control perspective because process control and incremental process improvement are best provided by those who have ownership of the process and are responsible for executing the steps. Juxtaposed to this is the set of program controls put in place by upper management to establish accountability and ensure consistent performance across projects. Just as over-specification is to be avoided in the design process, program controls must allow for individual differences in project needs. The definitions of some controls need to be delegated to the individual projects. Distinct processes are needed, each well-defined and having uniform execution, but with some flexibility in determination of application.

Standards form the basis by which processes, projects, programs, and products can be measured, evaluated, and controlled. The discussion of quality management's role (in Chapter 7) will provide a further discussion of standards.

1.5 A HANDBOOK OVERVIEW

This book has been designed to assist the responsible software engineering manager by presenting its topics in the following order.

Chapter 2, "Program Framework:"
- for viewing product realization projects
- for viewing process improvement projects
- for delineating reviews and audits

Chapter 3, "Project Reviews:"
- defines a "management review process" for project and program reviews
- provides identification and discussion of the greatest project review application needs (concept closure, project definition and funding, product realization, trial readiness, and general market availability)
- discusses the challenge of implementing a program of project reviews

Chapter 4, "Product Reviews:"
- provides distinct process definitions for popular product reviews (the technical review, software inspection, and walkthrough processes)
- discusses the challenge of implementing a program of product reviews

Chapter 5, "Auditing:"
- defines an "audit process" that can be used for product, process, project, and program evaluations
- identifies and discusses prominent audit application needs (the quality system audit, in-process audits to confirm procedural adherence, functional audits, and physical configuration audits)
- discusses the challenges of auditing

Chapter 6, "Special Topics:"
- to improve interviewing skills
- to increase the effectiveness of your reports
- to provide a taxonomy for the role of quality management

Chapter 7, "A Guess and a Vision:"
- to help your program succeed

Appendixes:
- contain numerous checklists, forms, letters, and reports to provide a starting point in developing documents to meet your specific needs

An index is provided at the back of the handbook for those who wish to consult specific topics.

CHAPTER 2

Program Framework

Software development has exhibited both product (quality) and process (productivity) problems. Although a wide variety of methods have been administered to cure development ailments, no single treatment has proven adequate. A framework is provided here to usher in the controlled application of reviews and audits as proven software engineering techniques.

Every program should include projects from two distinct categories: (1) product realization and (2) process improvement. These two project categories are taken, in turn, and unfolded to provide a framework for applying reviews and audits. Reviews and audits are then compared and contrasted.

As already stated, there are four perspectives from which review and audit activities can be considered: product, process, project, and program. Some examples of review and audit activities categorized by perspective include:

- Product
  Functional Audit
  Physical (configuration) Audit
  Technical review of the requirements specification
- Process
  In-process audit of inspections
  Walkthrough of problem report escalation procedures
  Inspection of process descriptive (or prescriptive) documents
- Project
  Project reviews (such as concept closure, project definition)
  Software Verification & Validation Plan review
  Financial and managerial accounting audits

- Program
  Quality Systems Audit (quality program evaluation)
  Management review of progress against business plans

Project reviews, product reviews, and audits are discussed at length in preparation for chapters by the same name. Presentation of specific processes and their application are left to those chapters.

2.1 PRODUCT REALIZATION

Whether your organization describes its development activities using the classical waterfall model (that is, life-cycle) or touts spiral, or evolutionary delivery, three macro-model elements prevail:

- Process definition
- Process control
- Process environment

Together they provide a framework for communicating, evaluating, and controlling software development. Process definition (i.e., process model) comprises those descriptive or prescriptive statements of how the development effort is to proceed, and process controls are designed to make it happen. For completeness, we acknowledge issues beyond our immediate span of control so those "process environment" issues can be understood and handled.

This discussion of process definition, control, and environment applies to both new product introduction efforts and maintenance. It is left for the readers to determine whether the activity sets for new product introduction and maintenance should be handled separately or integrated into the same macro-model for their company. Either scenario is workable. In fact, the modeling of maintenance activities follows the approach taken here for new product introduction. Maintenance can require anything up to the rigor required for new product development. Three classes of activity, listed by increased effort, are corrective maintenance, perfective maintenance, and adaptive maintenance, Corrective maintenance is required to provide fixes. Perfective maintenance can provide enhanced performance or functionality. Adaptive maintenance represents a major redevelopment effort to adapt an established product to changing marketplace needs.

This macro-model discussion is provided to set a framework for software development that facilitates the discussion of software reviews and audits, and it is therefore limited in this text to a focus on software. It can and should, however, be expanded to include all products and services that constitute the delivered system. Clearly this includes, but is not limited to, software, firmware, hardware, and documentation. Documentation is frequently viewed as a software element in today's industry. Firmware tends to be developed as software but maintained and serviced as hardware.

2.1.1 Process Definition

Difficulty in describing the model implies diminished likelihood that you can repeat the process with consistent results. A development model description, regardless of the model used, should contain the following elements:

- A detailed description of the deliverables of each step (such as phase, process step, or state)
- The type and ordering of activities required to complete the step and produce the desired deliverables
- The type, ordering, and coordination of verification and validation (V&V) activities within the process step that support the overall verification and validation objectives
- The organizational design and assignment of responsibility for each activity and deliverable
- Customer and supplier involvement in specific process activities

Whether the school of thought that is prevalent in your organization considers reviews and audits as a methodology separate from (but still symbiotic with) V&V, or as one of its integral components, a planned and rigorous V&V approach is needed that covers both product and process verification and validation needs.

- A *product* is *validated* as being consistent with and mappable to the requirements specification (for example, code, as the implementation of the product's design, meets the intent of those product requirements apportioned to it by the design).
- A *product* is *verified* as being a reasonable and anticipated extension of its higher abstraction level (for example, code correctly and adequately implements the design).
- A *process* is *validated* as being consistent with and mappable to project requirements that lead to its application. For example, the inspection process may be considered validated as applied to code if its application has effectively reduced the number of serious defects reaching the test effort, as targeted by the verification and validation plan. This could be exhibited by a reduction in internal failure costs and a reduction in the number of defects identified by the test effort without decreasing the ratio of that number to the total number of defects found during the test effort and customer operations.
- A *process* is *verified* as having been an accurate and true execution as defined by the process description. For example, in-process audits may have verified that, when applied, the code inspection process is executed uniformly and consistent with the definition of the code inspection process.

Each major entity of your organization should be actively involved in V&V activities during each process step. To facilitate any managerial accounting that exists as part of your "cost of quality" program, quality cost components should be tracked and analyzed to identify possible process improvement projects (see Section 2.2). Verification and validation activities should be planned such that failure costs can be separated from prevention and appraisal costs.

Documentation also plays an important role in V&V. Software Verification and Validation Plans [IEEE 1012] can be written and reviewed to direct V&V efforts for a given project. Software verification diagrams can be required or recommended as supporting documentation for the test efforts. In addition, in-process development documentation, though more commonly associated with constructing than checking activities (V&V), contributes to reviews and audits in two important ways. First, standardizing the use and format of in-process documentation makes their review easier and more effective. This is predominantly a benefit of consistent format. Secondly, audit trails are made more evident.

2.1.2 Process Control

Project management, configuration management, and quality management are added as a second layer to lead, monitor, and control process execution for the project. Project reviews are held to help meet control objectives and audits can be used to verify in-process conformance to procedural requirements or product composition and function.

As the three components of process model control represent perspectives that are frequently in conflict, they must be of equal concern. Although this may appear a minor point, it is critical to organizing this book's content. These three control components are not assumed to be represented by three separate organizations. In fact, although an individual or organization may have responsibility and authority for a particular control component, the related control activities may require implementation contrary to organizational autonomy:

- Control-related efforts are integrated into the processes they control.
- Tools, workbenches, and environments can be formed around control objectives so that they contribute directly to consistency, repeatability, and audit trails.
- Some control authority is delegated across functions in the form of special boards or committees (change control board, quality committee, and so on).
- A "project controls" department may be formed to provide the necessary mechanics, as the three control components frequently rely on the same data. Development should not be bombarded by uncoordinated requests for the same data in different format.

Further, it is important to note that the development managers in your organization will have responsibility for some project management, configuration management, and quality management activities. Because the scope of these responsibilities varies greatly across the industry, we speak of the three control components in this text and do not specifically call out development management as providing any specific control. Since your company can be organized by function, project, or by some matrix, further readings on organizational design, and project structures is recommended [CLELAND, 1975, 1983].

Project management is the first control component added to the development framework. It directs efforts needed to advance the project through the V&V augmented process model. Critical activities include:

- Determining the required tasks and their schedule
- Defining the work-flow and the organization(s) responsible
- Monitoring and reporting progress
- Directing resources to meet project objectives

Navigating through the process model generates products at various levels of abstraction, completeness, and stability (rate of change). The configuration management control component is added to the development framework to ensure capture control, and communication of the product state. Critical configuration management activities include:

- Configuration item identification
- Change control
- Configuration auditing
- Configuration status accounting

The final control component is quality management leading activities to provide continuous improvement to ensure that products are of predictable quality, are on time, and are within budget. Information sources available to quality management include data from V&V activities, project-level and in-process audits, test verification reports, and information from the field.

Together these three components work to control the process model (Figure 2-1). The perspective from which these control elements view progress brings them into conflict, so confrontations are sure to arise. This occurs whether local implementation calls for distributed responsibilities or three distinct functional entities. As

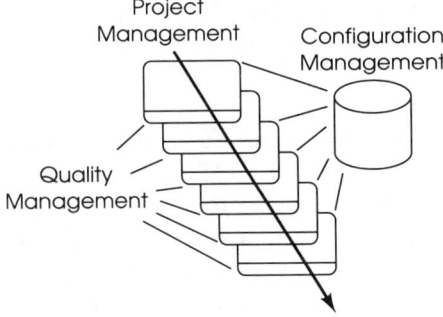

Figure 2-1 Process controls

PRODUCT REALIZATION 11

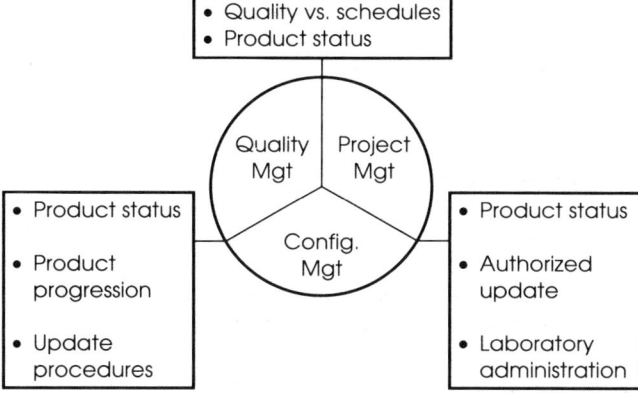

Figure 2-2 Control conflicts

an example, the conflict diagram (Figure 2-2) is used to depict some conflicting objectives. Quality versus schedules is a classic point of confrontation between project management and quality management.

To further accent how control component perspectives can vary, product status is identified in the diagram as a point of conflict:

- There is project management concern for whether the product is complete and reviewed. Formal publication of the software element is important.
- There is quality concern for review disposition and re-verification status. Publication of the element includes quality data reporting.
- Configuration management requires not only that the software element be completed, but *also* that any baseline updates be completed. Publication is viewed as including the availability (e.g., completed distribution) of the element.

We have seen how control components can be in conflict, but there is an interdependency as well. That interdependency is evidenced when activities related to one control component require timely execution of activities related to another. For example, the interpretation of productivity reports is aided by knowing the related quality statistics.

In addition, recall the discussion of controlled process evolution. Improvements for one component may require a particular level of technological maturity in the other control components. This maturity of each component relative to the others is important because the state of one control component can constrain evolution of the others. For example:

> Inspection process metrics analyzed and reported by the quality department can be of great value to project management. Known defect removal efficiencies against resources consumed is one important input to scheduling activities. Although scheduling and tracking efforts of project management may be mature enough to use these to advantage, the value (i.e., certainty) of the information

is diminished if the quality function does not perform in-process audits that verify uniform inspection process conformance. Moreover, if change control is not adequately rigorous, the inspection team's ability to identify defects is further impeded.

2.1.3 Process Environment

Because not everything is within our span of control, an environmental component is added to account for constraints such as those from geographic distribution of project responsibilities, organizational structures, reward mechanisms, or tool/workbench/environment availability. Periodic review of constraint management is suggested.

When an extensive examination of environmental issues is desired, you might include:

- Task Environment: This relates to issues encountered by the individual attempting to follow standard procedure. An example would be the lack of meeting facilities required to meet process model objectives. Inspections, as part of the process model, would suffer. Another example might be defect-laden test tools or workbenches that are driven past their normal capacity.
- Job Environment: This category is similar to the first, but encompasses the entire task set represented by a particular job description. An example is the frequent fate of software quality engineers as a result of annual ratings. Segregated into small, organizationally distributed teams, these engineers can be subject to stiff competition within their own ranks. Many companies then integrate their performance results into the local development universe where the software quality engineer traditionally fares poorly. If the function has been seen as a source of annoyance to development personnel during the year, its people lose further ground when integrated into the local universe. Another example is a job description written so as to require juggling too many accounts, interfaces, or tasks at the same time, which is clearly detrimental to performance. Excessive heat, cold, or noise in the environment could also fall within this category.
- Project Environment: Issues beyond direct control that are unique to a specific project fall in this category. One example is problems stemming from unreasonable or inflexible schedules. How the schedules came to be blessed in the first place is a control issue; resulting problems, if widespread and severe, are candidates for this category. Excessive overtime required on a project, as another example, not only generates frustration but directly affects productivity and quality of work. Geographic distribution of project responsibilities and other roadblocks to project communication belong here.
- Company Environment: Project and company environment categories are similar, with the latter knowing no project boundary. An example is the prevailing management style of the company, its commitment to equal opportunity, educational assistance, or professional development. Rewards not attuned to

process objectives would fit in this category. An entrepreneurial effort turned successful can exhibit growth pains, intensified power struggles, and other characteristics that provide other good examples.
- Business Environment: Market, financial, and related issues are representative of this category. This could include shrinking market windows, weaknesses in financial or managerial accounting techniques, or the company's financial situation. Customer expectations and competitive positioning are further examples.

2.2 PROCESS IMPROVEMENT

Product technology is understood and managed by most companies and is commonly acknowledged as an important product differential. Similarly, process technology should also be a focal point. Recall the Quality/Cost curve (Figure 2-3) that everyone references, but that apparently lacks impact in application. "Quality/Cost" is really a misnomer, because the curve itself is actually a reflection of process technology applied on a given project. In fact, the Japanese have not "inverted" the Quality Cost curve as many have observed; they only pursue the controlled migration (Figure 2-4) to increasingly better process technologies.

With software often accounting for nearly 80 percent of systems research and development (R&D), the importance of controlled process evolution should be apparent. Obviously it is not. Everyone has Problem Reporting and Corrective Action (PRCA) mechanisms in place for product problems; *process* PRCA is lacking.

Recall that software error costs increase throughout the life cycle (Figure 2-5) and that for telecommunications software, a defect removed after delivery to the field can cost 150 times what it would have cost to fix at requirements time. For larger systems, the problems are amplified. Perhaps this is why maintenance costs frequently outweigh development costs 2 to 1. Recent studies show maintenance costs as high as 80 percent of the total life cycle costs.

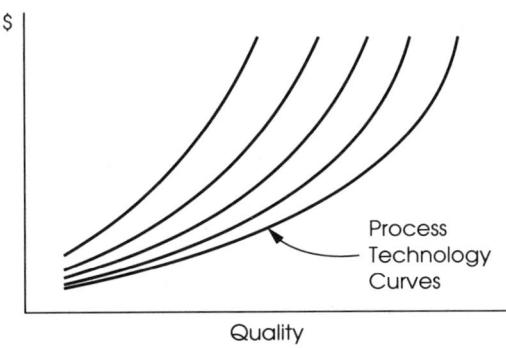

Figure 2-3 The "Quality Cost" family of curves

14 PROGRAM FRAMEWORK

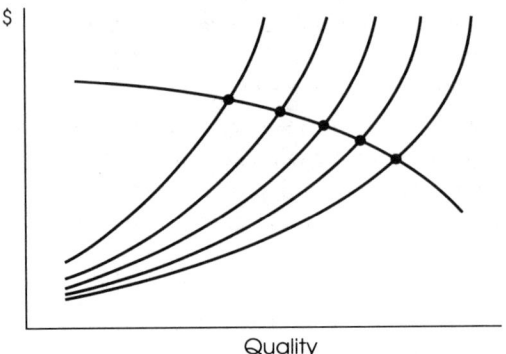

Figure 2-4 Apparent curve inversion

There is a need for a new emphasis on controlling process evolution. With new product technologies on the way, the need for new process technologies must be recognized. The ability to migrate to those new process technologies in an organized way is of great importance in achieving your vision. Failure there would directly affect margin.

To further illustrate this point, consider that future maintenance costs are committed with every dollar spent on development. Given the common 2 to 1 ratio discussed earlier, 20 cents per year is committed to maintenance for every development dollar spent. This is based on a ten-year, straight-line amortization of the two maintenance dollars attracted. The yearly obligation increases where product life is projected to be less than ten years. Figure 2-6 shows revenue and cost issues overlaid onto our framework.

A program of selected projects and their processes is managed to create a marketable solution system comprising products and services. The anticipated advance of technology (that is, *product* technology) is relied on to provide new products and services adequate to increase market share and to enter new markets. The cost side, a function of process technology, is overshadowed.

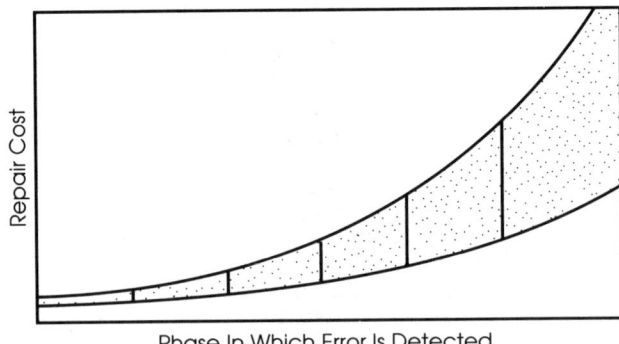

Figure 2-5 Software error costs increase throughout the life cycle

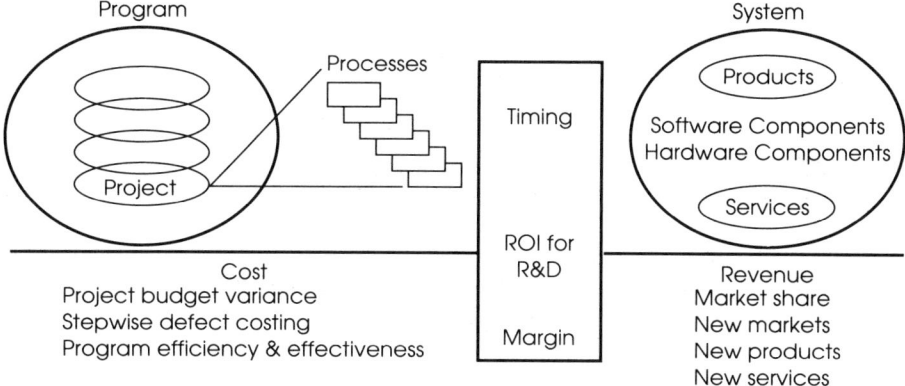

Figure 2-6 Cost and revenue as related to the framework

It is unreasonable to expect future margins comparable to today's unless process technology is controlled and evolved. Return on investment (ROI) for research and development and responsiveness to the marketplace depend on the technology-based cost issues of defect costing, project budget variance, and the overall effectiveness and efficiency of the program.

2.2.1 Controlling Improvement

A typical improvement project within this framework would exhibit major milestones (see project checklists in the appendixes) similar to the following:

- Project sponsorship
- Cause definition
- Remedy identification and trial readiness
- Remedy proven
- Remedy transitioned

Notice the similarities to new product development and its management structure. There are general managers responsible for guiding the overall development effort, project managers responsible for guiding specific projects, and researchers and engineers responsible for doing the detailed work. Indeed, these milestones are used in the next chapter to present process improvement project reviews.

For process improvement, program leadership is typically provided by a steering committee concerned with:

- Managing an effective mix of individual process improvement projects
- Providing training and guidance for process improvement and cost reduction
- Assuring visibility, recognition, and support

A typical joint program review meeting may include, but is not limited to:

- A presentation of the progress made on each project since the previous session
- Scheduled training and its implications for the projects
- Agreement on steps to be taken in support of the projects
- Agreement on how to continue managing the overall improvement program

A project team exists to tackle each improvement project as part of the overall program and has a member, usually the leader, on the Program Steering Committee. The team leader's major responsibilities are to:

- Manage the administrative details of the project approach.
- Identify project objectives with the help of the Pareto analysis.
- Screen the nominated project objectives and establish priorities.
- Provide for review by middle managers.
- Sell, in turn, the project proposal, the findings, and the resulting process improvement to management.

Because of differences between activities before and after cause definition, a planned change in leadership after that project review is not uncommon. Often a project chairperson and co-chairperson will switch roles at that point.

Each project team has a secretary to assist in project administration. For some projects it may be useful to bring in a specialist who is knowledgeable in quality-oriented concepts and skilled in using related tools. This specialist (or resource leader) provides consulting assistance to the project team and may come from the steering committee or quality department.

Regular project reports are required to:

- Ensure that the project team has a consensus understanding of project status and direction
- Keep all interested parties informed; the steering committee would typically approve the distribution list
- Record findings for later evaluation

Reports are normally drafted by the project secretary after each meeting and then reviewed by the project leader. These reports can provide:

- A record of progress and participation
- A list of discussion items or theories about cause and effect
- Process or product flow diagrams or other documentation useful to participants or the development area in general
- A documented analysis of symptoms or the results of tests performed
- Conclusions and recommendations reached

- Results achieved (both tangible and intangible)
- Current constraints or limitations
- Further plans and action items

2.2.2 Supporting Improvement

Senior management commitment and participation at the lowest levels of decision making is essential. Visibility of the team and individual contributions, acknowledgement and action by management, and reward attuned to process objectives are all important elements of an environment conducive to process improvement.

2.3 REVIEW AND AUDIT TAXONOMY

The *IEEE Standard Glossary of Software Engineering Terminology* [IEEE, 729] defines a review as:

1. A formal meeting at which a product or document is presented to the user, customer, or other interested parties for comment and approval. It can be a review of the management and technical progress of the hardware/software development project.
2. The formal review of an existing or proposed design for the purpose of detection and remedy of design deficiencies that could affect fitness-for-use and environmental aspects of the product, process, or service, and/or for identification of potential improvements of performance, safety, or economic aspects.

The first definition provides a framework for a genus (reviews) of examinations that can be applied to both products and projects. The second definition has a more technical emphasis and suggests a "technical review" process of broad application scope. Managerial reviews are seen as applying to projects and overall programs, whereas technical reviews pertain to products.

The *IEEE Standard Glossary of Software Engineering Terminology* [IEEE, 729] defines audit as:

1. An independent review for the purpose of assessing compliance with software requirements, specifications, baselines, standards, procedures, instructions, codes, and contractual and licensing requirements.
2. An activity to determine through investigation the adequacy of, and adherence to, established procedures, instructions, specifications, codes, and standards or other applicable contractual and licensing requirements, and the effectiveness of implementation. (ANSI N45.2.10-1973)

The major distinction to be drawn between reviews and audits, as two separate examination classes, is that audits are independently managed by a central figure (i.e., the auditor) who has complete authority and ownership of the audit and resulting reports, yet has no direct control over the corrective actions taken by the audited organization.

Audits, similar in many ways to other examinations, differ in independence and authority (Figure 2-7). These two examination attributes are closely related. With independence comes absolute authority on the execution of the contracted audit but no authority to mandate any corrective course or plan of action, as represented in quadrant IV of Figure 2-7. Change is owned by the controlling or contracting entity. Independence fuels the audit team's ability to access needed information and work elements and to report objectively against predefined audit criteria. Further distinctions include:

- *The mechanism.* Reviews rely on a meeting protocol.
- *Duration.* Audits may take months as compared to the few hours required by reviews.
- *Initiation.* Reviews are typically held in reaction to a specific project milestone or process step, as prescribed in program standards or project level planning documents. Audits, on the other hand, are not tied to the development process so much as to its controls.

Commonalities include:

- *Structure.* Audits rely on the existence of objective audit criteria (e.g., contracts, requirements, plans, specifications, standards) against which software elements and processes can be evaluated. Similarly, review examinations rely on the existence of standards for content and format (as in product reviews) and standard procedures and control (as in project reviews).
- *Nesting.* Reviews may require multiple meeting sessions to cover required materials. Audits can include other audit activities, reviews held by the auditors, and independent testing performed or contracted by the auditors.

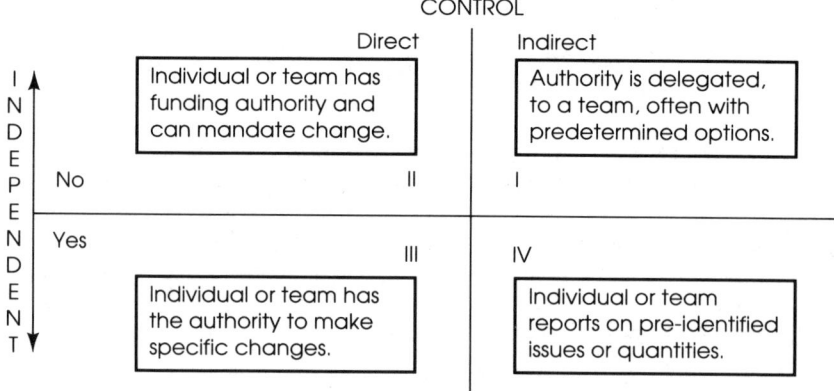

Figure 2-7 Some distinctions: Reviews *versus* audits

Look once again at Figure 2-7. Each quadrant of the chart represents a unique mixture of authority and independence that can help us understand the differences between various review and audit applications:

Quadrant I: Indirect Control, Project Dependent. Authority is delegated to a team, often with predetermined options. This situation is representative of most product review activity. The most pronounced example is the use of the inspection process where product disposition is selected by the team from three distinct options. Product reviews performed as part of an audit retain project independence and fall in Quadrant IV.

Quadrant II: Direct Control, Project Independent. An individual or the team has the authority to initiate, modify or withdraw funding. Change is mandated. This is best exemplified by an executive review team examining program content and progress. They have independence from the projects reviewed and wield financial power. That power, however, is difficult to focus and although change can be mandated, the specific details of change are left to those in a position of project responsibility.

Quadrant III: Direct Control, Project Dependent. An individual or the team has the authority to make specific changes according to program standards. A project review by the manager having profit and loss responsibility for that project is representative of this mixture of control and dependence.

Quadrant IV: Indirect Control, Project Independence. An individual or team reports on preidentified issues or quantities. Audits reside in this quadrant. Industry has exhibited some confusion between audits and management reviews. Independence from, and the lack of direct control over the product, process, or project examined are key attributes of an audit that are not shared by any review process.

2.3.1 Project Reviews

Reviews are held to help meet control objectives for each project. These are held with great inconsistency across the industry. As the purpose emphasized here is control, perhaps the single greatest difference is whether or not the manager responsible for profit and loss resides over the review. In many cases that manager's direct reports manage the review as a team and hold the decision-making authority, albeit subject to executive veto.

A project review is a formal management-team evaluation of a project-level plan or a project's status relative to such a plan. Product line management, project management, or a project controls group typically provides the necessary mechanics. The review team communicates progress, coordinates the decision making within their span of control, and provides recommendations for:

- Making activities progress according to plan, based on an evaluation of product development status
- Changing project direction or identifying the need for alternative planning
- Maintaining global control of the project through adequate allocation of resources

Typical product realization project milestones subject to management review include:

- Concept closure
- Project definition
- Product realization
- Trial readiness
- General market availability
- Product maturity
- Product retirement

2.3.2 Product Reviews

A program of formal product reviews is attractive because it addresses the diseconomies of scale [BOEHM, 1981] that contribute to the disproportionately increased costs on a large project (Figure 2-8). Product reviews can be used to focus on Boehm's issues and minimize cost differences in the following ways:

- Design specification rework is reduced by guiding the design activity to focus on defect removal.
- Verification emphasis is migrated to the earliest application of proven examination techniques.
- Change control and consistency of representation is provided for communicating both product and process interface issues.
- Integration activity effectiveness is improved through early verification of architecture and interfaces.
- The test function is freed to concentrate on a destructive test philosophy by minimally ensuring an acceptable quality level in the arriving product. Moreover, having participated in design reviews and in the review of their own test plans, the test team significantly improves their contribution to product quality.

Technical review, inspection, and walkthrough are the three process alternatives presented in this book to meet the need for product reviews.

The walkthrough, according to the *IEEE Standard Glossary of Software Engineering Terminology* [IEEE, 729] is:

> A software engineering review process in which a designer or programmer leads one or more members of the development team through a segment of design or code that he or she has written, while other members ask questions and make comments about technique, style, possible errors, violation of the development standards, and other problems.

Wide recognition for documenting the walkthrough process goes to Edward Yourdon [YOURDON, 1978]. Gerald Weinberg [FREEDMAN, 1982] [WEINBERG,

> More design is required to develop the unit-level specifications that support the parallel activity of a larger programming staff.
>
> More effort is required to verify and validate the larger requirements and design specifications.
>
> Even with a thoroughly defined specification, programmers on a large project will spend more time communicating and resolving interface issues.
>
> More integration activity is required to put the units together.
>
> In general, more extensive testing is required to verify and validate the software product.

Figure 2-8 Boehm's dis-economies of scale

1984] is generally credited with furthering the concept of the walkthrough with his "egoless programming" and "egoless technical reviews."

Michael Fagan has prescribed the Software Inspection Process [FAGAN, 1976, 1977] to focus the examination process back to project controls. Similar to the walkthrough process, inspecting provides several additional benefits at increased overhead. That investment, however, is swiftly returned in the form of improved process control and reduced rework downstream. The key benefits, as summarized by Fagan [1977] are that "inspections increase productivity and improve final program quality. Furthermore, improvements in process control and project management are enabled by inspections".

The inspection, according to the *IEEE Standard Glossary of Software Engineering Terminology* [IEEE, 729] is:

1. A formal evaluation technique in which software requirements, design, or code are examined in detail by a person or group other than the originator to detect faults, violation of development standards, and other problems.
2. A phase of quality control that by means of examination, observation, or measurement determines the conformance of materials, supplies, components, parts, systems, processes, or structures to predetermined quality requirements.

The latter definition clearly relates to the inspections used in manufacturing, where a multitude of like units are produced and a representative sample is examined. If we were to form an analogy with software development, we would see a multitude of distinct units. For each unit inspected, there would be a 100 percent sample rate. This is true because the sample size of one is the same as the number produced.

Having seen the walkthrough and inspection as two "species" of review, we start to make the transition to defining their genus. According to the *IEEE Standard Glossary of Software Engineering Terminology* [IEEE, 729] a review is:

1. A formal meeting at which a product or document is presented to the user, customer, or other interested parties for comment and approval. It can be a review of the management and technical progress of the hardware/software development project.

2. The formal review of an existing or proposed design for the purpose of detection and remedy of design deficiencies that could affect fitness-for-use and environmental aspects of the product, process, or service, and/or for identification of potential improvements of performance, safety, or economic aspects.

Here we see the first definition providing a framework for a genus of examinations (that is, reviews). The second definition has a more technical emphasis and suggests an additional "technical review" process of wider application scope than the walkthrough or inspection. Detailed process descriptions are provided in Chapter 4.

2.3.3 Audits

We have already seen that an audit is an activity to determine, through investigation, the adequacy or adherence to established procedures or specifications. Audits, similar in many ways to other examinations, differ from them in independence and authority. With independence comes absolute authority on the execution of the contracted audit but no authority to mandate any corrective course or plan of action. Change is owned by the controlling or contracting entity.

There is a definitive framework for audit partitioning. That framework, as represented in the following definitions, however, has audits partitioned by application (the subject of the activity) rather than by any audit process distinctions.

Product Quality Audit. A quantitative assessment of conformance to required product characteristics [ANSI, 1978].

Process Quality Audit. An evaluation of elements of a process and appraisal of completeness, correction of conditions, and probable effectiveness [ANSI, 1978].

Quality Systems Audit. A documented activity performed to verify by examination and evaluation of objective evidence that applicable elements of the quality system are suitable and have been developed, documented, and effectively implemented in accordance with specified requirements [ANSI, 1978].

Owing to this lack of process distinction between audit applications, the approach has been taken here to provide a single procedural definition for audits in general, and then to discuss specific application needs (see Chapter 5).

Success in meeting application needs, however, typically depends on the following prerequisites:

- Objective audit criteria exist (e.g., contracts, requirements, plans, specifications, standards) against which software elements and processes can be evaluated.
- Audit personnel are selected to promote team objectivity. They are usually independent of any direct responsibility for the products and processes examined and may be from an external organization.

- Audit personnel are given sufficient authority by appropriate management personnel to perform the audit.

2.4 SUMMARY

Every program should include projects from two distinct categories: (1) product realization and (2) process improvement. Reviews and audits play a significant role in the controls and inner workings of both product realization projects and process improvement projects.

The three components of process technology that require continuous improvement are the process model, controls placed on the model, and the environment in which the model and its controls reside. The process model includes all methodologies and techniques of development as individual areas for improvement as well as provides an opportunity to improve the effectiveness and efficiency of the mixture of methodologies and techniques applied. Here, product reviews are part of the process. Project reviews and audits help control the process.

Catching problems as early as possible is the emphasis of reviews and audits. Whether the defects are in the specification of requirements, in the design, in the code, or in the way we go about the business of software development, earlier identification and removal means dollars saved.

CHAPTER 3

Project Reviews

Project reviews are held to help meet control objectives and to provide a management-team evaluation of a project-level plan or a project's status relative to such a plan. This applies to both product realization and process improvement. This chapter provides a suitable project review process and further discusses its application and the challenges facing the practitioner.

3.1 MANAGEMENT REVIEW PROCESS

3.1.1 Objective

A *management review* is a formal management-team evaluation of a project-level plan or a project's status relative to such a plan. The review team communicates progress, coordinates the decision making within their span of control and provides recommendations for:

- Making activities progress according to plan, based on an evaluation of product development status
- Changing project direction or identifying the need for alternative planning
- Maintaining global control of the project through adequate allocation of resources

Moreover, to further tailor this review process for an individual project milestone, specific objectives are to be identified in a "Statement of Objectives" made available before the review meeting. Typical objective sets will be presented later in this chapter and extended checklists are made available in the appendixes. If critical data and information cannot be supplied, then an additional meeting is typically scheduled to complete the management review process. The management review concept can be applied to new development or to maintenance activities. It can also be useful in managing process improvement projects (see Section 2.2).

3.1.2 People and Their Agendas

Roles for the management review include:

- Leader
- Reporter
- Team member

The review leader is responsible for the administrative tasks pertaining to the review, for assuring that the review is conducted in an orderly manner, and for issuing any minutes or reports. The reporter is responsible for having the project status and all supporting documentation available for distribution before the meeting. This individual is also responsible for documenting the findings, decisions, and recommendations of the review team.

Each member of the review team is responsible for being adequately prepared for the meeting and assuring that the review meets its objectives.

3.1.3 When to Hold a Management Review

Typically, the project planning documents (for example, Software Quality Assurance Plan, Software Development Plan, or Software Verification and Validation Plan) establish the need for conducting specific management reviews. As stated in these plans, a management review can be initiated by the completion of a project phase or specific software deliverable (for example, a planning document, a requirements specification, or a design document). Moreover, management reviews not required by plan may occur, as needed, to deal with any unscheduled events or contingencies.

A selected review leader establishes or confirms a statement of objectives for the meeting and verifies that any appropriate software deliverables and any other documents or reports are available and sufficiently complete to support the review objectives. In addition to any applicable reference material supplied by project management, or requested by the review leader, these would include:

- A Statement of Objectives for the management review and its agenda
- Current project schedule, resource, and cost data
- Pertinent reports (for example, managerial review reports, technical review reports, or audit reports) from other reviews and/or audits already completed
- Software deliverable status or current disposition

3.1.4 Procedures

The review leader, having identified the team, schedules facilities for the meeting and distributes any materials needed by the review team for advanced preparation (for example, statement of objectives, agenda, or presentation requirements). In addition, the review leader might consider requesting that a project representative conduct an overview session for the review team. This overview can occur as part of the examination meeting or as a separate meeting. It is critical that each individual on the review team studies the material and prepares for the review meeting.

During the management review the review team holds one or more meetings to examine project status and determine if it complies with pre-defined plans and standards, and records all deviations and associated risk assessments.

Constraints, whether internal or external, are discussed with emphasis on those factors not originally considered in the project plan. A list of issues and recommendations is generated for the attention of the next management level. This may include additional reviews or audits. A general course of action is set (or recommended) commensurate with the team's authority, and action items are defined and assigned.

Although plan adjustments or product rework may result from the management review they are not considered part of the process, except where needed to complete the current examination. The management review process is considered complete when all issues identified in the review "Statement of Objectives" have been addressed and the management review report has been issued. Project management typically tracks any action items through to resolution. If a re-review is required, it would provide confirmation of action item completion.

3.1.5 Output

The Management Review Report identifies:

- The project being reviewed and the team that participated in that review
- Inputs to the review
- Review objectives
- Action item ownership, status, and tracking responsibility
- Project status and a list of issues that must be addressed for the project to meet its milestone
- Recommendations regarding any further reviews and audits, and a list of additional information and data that must be obtained before they can be executed

3.2 SPECIFIC PROCESS APPLICATIONS

3.2.1 Project Reviews for Product Realization

Typical product realization project milestones include:

- Concept closure
- Project definition
- Product realization

- Trial readiness
- General market availability
- Product maturity
- Product retirement

In addition, any point in the project where prime responsibility or project emphasis shifts is a further candidate milestone for applying the management review process. Other applications may include a follow-up or "postmortem" view of any project phase. The review of product mix strategy, product performance, and position to market might prove helpful in determining whether product retirement is appropriate and, if so, how it might be gracefully removed from the market to minimize the company's liability.

This section discusses the use of the management review process to mark each of these milestones. A sample Statement of Objectives is provided for each, and related project checklists can be found in Appendix 1. Project reviews should not be confused with weekly project status meetings.

3.2.1.1 Concept Closure Holding a project review to mark *concept closure* verifies a proper precommitment analysis and avoids premature investment in new business. Only new business proposals (for example, new product development, major adaptive maintenance, or joint ventures) that exhibit a preliminary "winning strategy" receive funding to continue product and project definition. A statement of objectives for this project review might include confirmation that:

- The envisioned product is documented.
- The product is technically feasible.
- Financial targets have been established.
- Project controls are outlined.
- Product strategy is sound.

3.2.1.2 Project Definition Holding a project review to mark *project definition* verifies the definition and controls needed to proceed toward product realization. General product requirements have been documented and reviewed after strategic product planning that examined:

- Market requirements
- Competitive position
- Overall system or product family requirements
- Sales potential

In addition to product planning that identified what we want, project planning is verified as providing a means for getting what we want. A statement of objectives for this project review might include confirmation that:

- The product definition is adequate.
- The development process is in place.

- Financial targets have been refined.
- Project controls are detailed.
- Market strategy is sound.
- Market roll-out is planned.
- Competitive analysis has been completed and any resulting revisions to plans have been initiated and approved.
- Necessary training has been identified.
- The availability of adequate tools, workbenches, and environments has been planned.

3.2.1.3 Product Realization Holding a project review to mark *product realization* verifies a stable baseline for independent test activities. This requires that the product, as built, is an executable software system, complete with documentation, and that system-level test plans and procedures have all been reviewed in preparation for testing activities before any external product trial. A statement of objectives for this project review might include confirmation that:

- The delivered product meets its specifications.
- The delivered product is complete.
- Prescribed procedures were followed.
- Financial targets are on track.
- Project controls were correctly implemented.
- Product strategy is sound.

3.2.1.4 Trial Readiness Holding a project review to mark *trial readiness* verifies the quality and the completeness of the product offering needed to enter into external trials and the readiness of those support and control mechanisms required for a successful trial. A statement of objectives for this project review might include confirmation that:

- The specification framework is complete and current.
- Post-verification problem report status is acceptable.
- Prescribed procedures were followed.
- Product verification has been completed.
- The product is baselined and controlled.
- Manufacturing channel preparation is adequate.
- Delivery/service channel preparation is adequate.
- A reasonable evaluation mechanism is in place to judge against trial success criteria.
- Financial targets are on track.
- Project controls were correctly implemented.
- A trial plan has been reviewed and approved.

- The market strategy is sound.
- Sales channel preparation is adequate.
- Trial success criteria have been set.

3.2.1.5 General Market Availability Holding a project review to mark *general market availability* verifies the quality and the completeness of deliverable products and services and the readiness of all business channels to support general release. A statement of objectives for this project review might include confirmation that:

- The specification framework is complete and current.
- Post-trial problem report status is acceptable.
- Prescribed procedures were followed.
- Product trial has been completed.
- The product is baselined and controlled.
- Manufacturing channel preparation is adequate.
- Delivery/service channel preparation is adequate.
- Financial targets are on track.
- Project controls were correctly implemented.
- The market strategy is sound.
- Sales channel preparation is adequate.

3.2.1.6 Product Maturity Review Hold periodic project reviews to verify product maturity and to examine results against business expectations. This provides information that will assure timely retirement planning and update our understanding of product mix and performance. A statement of objectives for this project review might include confirmation that:

- The specification framework is complete and current.
- Product quality is stable and acceptable.
- Prescribed procedures are routinely followed.
- The product baseline remains under control.
- Manufacturing channel response is adequate.
- Delivery/service channel response is adequate.
- Financial targets are on track.
- Maintenance controls are correctly implemented.
- Operational support is adequate.
- The market strategy is sound.
- Sales channel response is adequate.

3.2.1.7 Product Retirement Review Holding a *product retirement review* when indicated by a mature product review or other business strategies can minimize disruption and avoid excessive costs (or lost opportunity). Completion of the review marks either approval of special funding for gracefully discontinuing the sales of a product and its support, redirecting the product's position through initiating adaptive maintenance, or the deferral of retirement. A statement of objectives for this project review might include confirmation that:

- The specification framework is deteriorating.
- The maintenance backlog is unacceptable.
- Prescribed procedures are breaking down.
- The product baseline is becoming vague.
- Manufacturing channel demand or response has slowed.
- Delivery/service channel resources are strained.
- Maintenance controls are faltering.
- The market strategy is being reexamined.
- Sales channel activity has diminished.

3.2.2 Project Reviews for Process Improvement

Typical process improvement project milestones include:

- Project sponsorship
- Cause definition
- Remedy identification and trial readiness
- Remedy proven
- Remedy transitioned

This section discusses the use of the management review process to mark each of these milestones. A sample Statement of Objectives is provided for each, and related project checklists can be found in Appendix 1. Project reviews in this category are typically attended by a steering committee comprising product realization project managers who have a chartered responsibility for process improvement. Together they fund the improvement projects and reap the rewards of continuous process improvement.

3.2.2.1 Project Sponsorship The successful completion of a project sponsorship review is a milestone that marks the legitimacy, rights, and responsibilities of a process improvement project team. A statement of objectives for this project review might include confirmation that:

- A team has been formed.
- The team's charter documents work objectives and plans.
- Funding and resource needs have been identified.
- The proposed effort is feasible and consistent with overall program objectives.
- The proposed effort can be accomplished within current program constraints.

A team charter documents the team's authority and obligation to:

- Manage the team's resources.
- Report progress and resource use.
- Access and collect data.
- Perform analysis.
- Theorize cause and effect.
- Design and execute experiments and tests.
- Recommend corrective action.
- Recommend perfective action.
- Track improvement progress.
- Evaluate and publish results.

3.2.2.2 Cause Definition The successful completion of a cause definition review is a milestone that marks the completion of initial analysis and the beginning of synthesis. The team is ready to design a process solution. A statement of objectives for this project review might include confirmation that:

- The team has followed its authorized charter.
- Adequate research and analysis have been completed.
- With high probability, causal connectedness has been established.
- An initial plan for solution design has been documented.
- Any required changes have been made in team management.
- The effort remains feasible and consistent with overall program objectives and its initiating charter.
- The effort can continue within current program constraints.

Some defects are controllable by management, while others are within the span of control of individual members of the technical staff. Each of these two defect classes requires its own unique process improvement approach.

Diagnosis of process control defects (that is, those controllable by management) requires that we study our technology and our managerial practices. Once we discover the causes, solutions typically involve changes in technology and managerial practices. In contrast, diagnosis of process model related defects requires that we study work habits and the ability to perform within the established process descriptions and constraints. The remedies usually involve changes in staff member practices and priorities, have a quicker return on investment, and are best implemented by the people involved.

3.2.2.3 Remedy Identification and Trial Readiness The successful completion of a remedy identification and trial readiness review is a milestone that marks the completion of the process research and development effort authorized by the original team charter. The team is ready to submit its process solution for trial use. A statement of objectives for this project review might include confirmation that:

- The team has followed its authorized charter.
- With high probability, the new or improved process will provide a cost-effective solution that is compatible with the overall process mix and adequately addresses the problem(s) identified in the initiating charter.
- A first application of the new process or improvement has been identified and a trial plan has been documented.
- The effort remains feasible and consistent with overall program objectives and its initiating charter.
- The effort can continue within current program constraints.

3.2.2.4 Remedy Proven The successful completion of a remedy proven review is a milestone that marks the completion of the trial effort. Results have been reviewed and, where appropriate, a course of action has been outlined for wider process implementation or availability. A statement of objectives for this project review might include confirmation that:

- The trial plan has been adequately implemented.
- The trial results indicate that the new or improved process provided a cost-effective solution for the trial in the indicated area.
- Technology transfer issues have been adequately identified and studied.
- A realistic transition plan has been documented.

3.2.2.5 Remedy Transitioned The successful completion of a remedy transitioned review is a milestone that marks the general availability of the new or improved process and the existence of effective technology transfer assistance. A statement of objectives for this project review might include confirmation that:

- The transition plan has been successfully implemented and the new or improved process is an integrated part of the overall process mix.
- Any resulting changes to fine-tune the solution or the process have been approved, implemented, and verified effective.
- Gains have been consolidated.

3.3 THE IMPLEMENTATION CHALLENGE

We have already seen a suitable review process defined and have discussed its application in both product realization and process improvement projects. The definition, operation, and maintenance of a project review program has many challenges. Some are common to product realization and process improvement, others are unique to each. Key challenges include:

- Acceptance and participation
- Execution consistency
- Feedback

3.3.1 Acceptance and Participation

Know and make known what to expect is really the most important message. Whether for product realization or for process improvement, project reviews must exist as a program; individual review requirements must fit neatly together with a smooth progression of control issues over the project's duration. Determine first what you expect the review program to accomplish. Document, circulate, and achieve consensus for that expectation. The checklists in the appendixes can be used as a starting point for your editing. In addition, you should be sure to establish guidelines that still allow middle management some latitude in presenting their work status.

After figuring out what to expect from the review program, make sure people know what's expected of them. There should be clear meeting objectives, obvious and concerned ownership, and a standard meeting protocol. Meeting objectives are based on what you expect from the review program. Ownership should be exhibited and exercised by the person running the meeting. Meeting protocol will be discussed further in the section on execution consistency. For now, however, it is important to suggest that meetings open with a statement of objectives, a presentation of the agenda, and a roll call that includes introductions. The meeting should close with a statement consolidating all findings, a recommendation on how the project is to proceed, the project decision, and a preview of the next review session. Previewing the next review section is critical because it helps people understand what is expected of them well in advance and reinforces the review program. You can't have people entering a review told that they passed or failed unless they know in advance what the test is to be.

Participation and acceptance come more quickly when participants know to whom the meeting belongs, what the owner's objectives are, and how each individual is to contribute. This can be further enhanced by focusing on the project impact of work element status rather than on unnecessary detail within the work element. An example of this is determining whether contingencies can be established to compensate for deficiencies rather than dwelling on why those deficiencies exist and who might be blamed. Remember that the project fails if any project part fails: discussing blame is quite academic (Figure 3-1), and usually wrong, anyway. If the ship is sinking, fix the hole; don't discuss how it got there. Avoiding recurrence should be discussed later.

3.3.1.1 Unique Product Realization Issues
Stage fright can be a major phobia of middle management. In many organizations the maturity of process

Figure 3-1 The sinking ship

technology [Humphrey, 1989] is at the point where the overall process has some definition, but execution consistency is just starting to emerge. Interfaces and dependencies between elements of the organization are somewhat ad hoc, as they are defined by "whoever gets their job done first." And middle managers are told to get the job done. There's a natural and prevalent reluctance to bare related product deficiencies and discuss organizational interfaces. This contributes to stage fright when the middle mangers are confronted with the directive to participate in a project review that shifts the emphasis from their own areas to the health and welfare of the project as a whole. Middle managers from development then have their discomfort amplified by having to defend their work, not just from each other, but (heaven forbid) from people in other areas such as project management, manufacturing, installation and support, and training.

All this explains why the different areas tend to have their own dress rehearsals. Although these premeetings are not advisable, they are quite natural and represent an important step toward review acceptance. We want no rehearsals, but neither do we want any surprises.

Extra meetings will disappear as acceptance grows. To speed this migration from dress rehearsals and to reduce the fear of surprise, the project office, quality department, or whoever manages the review meetings should meet with key middle managers and help them integrate project review concerns into the regular meetings held in their own area during the course of each project step. This will help replace extra meetings during the week before the official review meeting.

As the review program progresses and individual acceptance increases, the overall tone of the meeting will shift from defending areas to open discussion of the project as a whole. More people will see the personal opportunity in active participation.

3.3.1.2 Unique Process Improvement Issues What if you gave a party and no one came? Or possibly worse, you threw several parties but were never quite able to gain acceptance? There is a strong analogy between this social nightmare and the surest assassin of process improvement projects: insufficient management exposure and response.

In addition to providing a program of management education on process improvement, the organization or individual responsible for facilitating the improvement projects should brief responsible management on the project, their decision-making role, and the general meeting protocol before each review is held. The outcome needs to be clear and any required follow-up needs to be verified.

3.3.2 Execution Consistency

Project planning is essential for the consistent execution of project reviews. As prerequisites to a successful review program, the following are also necessary to document the extent of your program's success or to take full advantage of your review investment:

- Standard entry and exit criteria should be defined for each project review.
- Development standards should provide for consistent product format and content, as well as define any product acceptance criteria.
- The project issues to be reviewed and the review process to be employed should be identified in program level standards.
- Support should be provided to the managerial staff in the execution of required reviews.
- Meeting protocol should be uniformly followed.

Although these are necessary for the success of your project review program, they are not sufficient. The need for execution consistency must be recognized. A clear policy statement regarding project reviews needs to be published and widely read. It should introduce control issues to be managed by the project review program and identify the required control points at which reviews are to be held. Procedurally, the project reviews must fit well into overall project methodology.

Meetings should be structured to support execution consistency and to minimize duration. Agendas and attendance requirements should be standardized. In application, review leaders should reschedule any review where representation is inadequate.

Presenters should be encouraged to report both the good and the bad. The added value of meetings where only good news is presented quickly deteriorates. Moreover, information and interpretation should be kept separate to allow isolation of the subjective evaluations from the objective observations. The meeting should not be the place to argue about numbers, although a healthy discussion of uncertainties and risks is quite typical.

Information doesn't make the decision, the management team does. Project disposition should not be left to some metric or heuristic. Decision-making authority and responsibility must be accepted by the management staff, and their decision should be documented with their signatures affixed.

3.3.2.1 Unique Product Realization Issues

Perhaps one of the most critical policy decisions required for product realization project reviews is whether:

- The review is to provide a decision-making mechanism with the "profit and loss" manager and key players in attendance, or
- The review is to provide a decision-making mechanism with the "profit and loss" manager delegating authority to key players who will act on his or her behalf during his or her absence.

If some mix of these two approaches is selected, it is critical that specific project review instances follow standard procedure for meeting ownership and results reporting.

Regardless of meeting ownership, it is important that the difference between process execution and managerial prerogative is understood. The management team has an obligation to follow the review process and determine project disposition according to local standards. The profit and loss manager has the authority, succumbing to business pressures, to have the project proceed contrary to review findings. This type of "business decision," however, needs to be kept separate from the review execution. As the decision maker is accountable for any deviation from recommended practice, any course of action contrary to the review outcome should be well documented. Proceeding in spite of known problems does not make the problems go away.

3.3.2.2 Unique Process Improvement Issues

Documented policies and procedures are just as important to process improvement as they are to product realization. The most important policy consideration is that working on an approved process improvement project is a sanctioned activity. Project participants should have their effort contracted from their functional organization to minimize staffing conflicts between the two project types they might serve. To manage this business within a business, formality must exist in proposing and managing individual improvement projects and in controlling the mix of projects as a single program for improvement. The quickest way to let execution consistency deteriorate is to allow product realization project pressures to interfere with the day to day improvement project efforts. Development issues will surely lead, but their influence should be constrained to contracting activities.

Written procedures are required to assign and delineate the facilitator (that is, program manager) role and to set general project responsibilities. As with product realization efforts, a strong program manager with known authority is essential. This is true not only for preserving contracts with the functional groups, but also for driving improvement project teams to project completion. The projects should not be allowed to wander from their approved Program Authorization Requests.

3.3.3 Feedback

Three areas where feedback can play an important role in program success include:

- Value of the Review. Does the review represent a visible step toward achieving control objectives as identified in program-level policy and procedures? Did information, as presented, add value to the decision-making process? Was the project disposition consistent with, and visibly flow from the information presented?
- Value of the Project. How does the consensus view of the project's value change as it progresses through the review program? Perspectives taken should include company, division, and team.
- Value of the Effort. Have project difficulties and individual contributions been recognized? Difficulties cannot indefinitely be met by extraordinary contribution. Eventually the cycle breaks down and the nth miracle never occurs.

Advice common to all three areas tells us to focus on project stages and to set success criteria for each as well as for the project as a whole. Such criteria should be SMART:

- **S**pecific: Both teams and participants need to know what is expected of them. Adequate detail is essential. Specification of product performance and early modeling activities can't be over-emphasized. The work breakdown structure should clearly map responsibilities to product parameters.
- **M**easurable: The presence of product parameters must be verifiable and it must be possible to gauge the extent of that presence in terms of specific acceptance criteria. Similarly, work performance must be measurable.
- **A**ttainable **R**esults: Feasibility studies are required to assure that product goals can be achieved. Staffing and process technology should be reviewed to ensure work results at the project, team, and individual levels. Skill management must ensure that the right person has the right assignment.
- **T**imely: The maturity of market analysis and the predictability of development are important in managing the project toward timely completion. Confidence is needed in our ability to meet a market window and confidence is required that the window exists as identified. The efforts of teams and individuals must progress along the planned schedule, with the critical path managed and contingencies planned.

3.3.3.1 Unique Product Realization Issues

Every company has its own culture, and how meetings are managed is part of that culture. The rigor required by project reviews may well be counter to that culture. Requiring attendance, starting on time, distributing a hard copy of presentations, rigorous control of action items, publishing minutes consistent in format and content, and signing off on a project disposition may present a culture shock to many in your organization. These review process requirements are, however, all important to establish feedback mechanisms that perform consistently. The foundation for this rigor should be documented in program policies and procedures. Further, review execution according to policies and procedures should be subject to audit. Only then can the following questions be answered with confidence:

- Have the appropriate organizational elements participated in the review process?
- Was consensus reached?
- Were conclusions consistent with the information presented?
- Is problem reporting and corrective action adequately visible and participatory?
- What activities are on the critical path?
- Have all significant contingencies adequately been planned for?
- Do people know what they are to do next?
- How do we recognize success for the project phase and for the project as a whole?

3.3.3.2 Unique Process Improvement Issues Staffing is one thing that makes managing process improvement projects unique. As people participate from across organizational boundaries, team leaders are left without any direct reports. Managing these teams takes on attributes of managing a volunteer work force, and this amplifies the need for feedback to reinforce participation and contribution. That feedback should include recognition, reward, and social status.

Team membership changes over time, with the most pronounced changes occurring as the project shifts from cause definition to remedy identification. This accents the need to maintain both feedback to those who have participated and a forward propagation of information to those most likely involved in subsequent efforts. Project authorization should be accompanied by requirements for maintaining key liaisons and for the distribution of meeting notices and reports.

A newsletter devoted to process improvement could identify active projects, discuss their status, recognize participants, and announce new efforts. It could also serve as a common source of information about current training and education opportunities, professional society activities, and scheduled conferences. Brief papers dealing with process issues could be solicited for publication.

Forming special interest groups can also be advantageous. These special interest groups, or SIGs, would assist interested parties in focusing in on specific elements of process technology (for example, systems analysis, performance modeling, or design specification). This ties in nicely with managing improvement projects because the SIGs might provide candidate projects and would certainly provide a resource pool for projects participation and review. They would have a vested interest in watching improvement projects and communicating their success.

3.4 SUMMARY

A clear policy statement regarding project reviews needs to be published and widely read. It should introduce control issues to be managed by the project review program and identify the required control points at which reviews are to be held. Procedurally, the project reviews must fit well into the overall project methodology. Participation and acceptance come more quickly when participants know to whom the meeting belongs, what the owner's objectives are, and how each individual is to contribute. As the review program progresses and individual acceptance increases, extra meetings (dress rehearsals) will disappear and the review meetings will see proactive project controls replace defensiveness.

Three areas where feedback can play an important role in program success include value of the review, value of the project, and value of the effort. Advice common to all three areas recommends focusing on project stages and setting success criteria for each and the project as a whole. Criteria should be aimed at judging specific, measurable results that are attainable and timely.

The rigor required by project reviews may well be counter to that culture. Requiring attendance, starting on time, distributing a hard copy of presentations, rigorous control of action items, publishing minutes consistent in format and content, and signing off on a project disposition may present a culture shock to many in your organization. These review process requirements are, however, all important to establish feedback mechanisms that perform consistently. The foundation for this rigor should be documented in program policies and procedures. Further, review execution according to policies and procedures should be subject to audit.

Perhaps one of the most critical policy decisions required for product realization project reviews is whether:

- The review is to provide a decision-making mechanism with the "profit and loss" manager and key players in attendance, or
- The review is to provide a decision-making mechanism with the "profit and loss" manager delegating authority to key players who will act on his or her behalf during his or her absence.

Regardless of meeting ownership, it is important that the difference between process execution and managerial prerogative is understood. The management team has an obligation to follow the review process and determine project disposition according to local standards. The profit and loss manager has the authority, succumbing to business pressures, to have the project proceed contrary to review findings. This type of "business decision," however, needs to be kept separate from the review execution. Information doesn't make the decision, the management team does. Project disposition should not be left to some metric or heuristic. Decision-making authority and responsibility must be accepted by the management staff and their decision should be documented with their signatures affixed.

There is a great need for management visibility and response in process improvement projects. Teams and individuals require evidence that their efforts are having an impact. The most important policy consideration is that working on an approved process improvement project is a sanctioned activity. A strong facilitator (that is, program manager) with known authority is needed to preserve contracts with functional groups and to drive efforts to completion according to their approved Program Authorization Requests.

Managing these teams takes on attributes of managing a volunteer work force, and this amplifies the need for feedback to reinforce participation and contribution. That feedback should include recognition, reward, and social status.

Team membership changes over time, with the most pronounced changes occurring as the project shifts from cause definition to remedy identification. This accents the need to maintain both feedback to those who have participated and a forward propagation of information to those most likely involved in subsequent efforts.

CHAPTER 4
Product Reviews

Product reviews have been a long-standing element of successful development programs. In this chapter, three distinct review processes suitable for product review application are presented. The technical review process is presented first. Presented as distinct derivatives formed by placing more restrictions (that is, changing process objectives) on the technical review process, the software inspection process and walkthrough process follow. In addition, application opportunities and process mix planning are discussed. This includes an example of where having multiple examinations using a variety of processes can prove beneficial. Review program acceptance and participation, execution consistency, and feedback are also discussed.

4.1 THE TECHNICAL REVIEW

4.1.1 Objective

The technical review process is used to evaluate a specific software element and provide evidence that the software element satisfies its specifications and conforms to applicable standards. It identifies deviations from standards and specifications and identifies defects.

Moreover, to further tailor this review process for an individual software element, specific objectives can be identified in a Statement of Objectives made available before the review meeting. The minimum statement of objectives is typically in the form of a checklist developed for a specific software element type used to assure that *its* objectives are met. This is common to all review processes, including this general review process, the inspection, and the walkthrough. It is also common to all review process applications. Examples of review process applications include the technical review, inspection, or walkthrough of a detailed design or test procedure.

A statement of objectives can include:

- Software Element Objectives. These focus on the software element reviewed.
- Verification and Validation (V&V) Objectives. This subset of possible objective statements focus on issues related to the V&V effort. Constraints imposed toward meeting V&V objectives represent distinctions between specific review processes, as will be seen in the discussion of inspections and walkthroughs.

Typical V&V objectives that suggest the use of this general technical review process include, but are not limited to:

- Providing wide exposure of the software element to the development universe
- Verifying that changes to the software element(s) affect only those system areas identified by the change specification
- Providing wide exposure of the software element to the development universe
- Acquiring a broad consensus on the design approach used or the software element itself

4.1.2 People and Their Agendas

Roles for the technical review include:

- Leader
- Scribe
- Team member

The review leader is responsible for conducting a specific review. This includes administrative tasks pertaining to the review and ensuring that the review is conducted in an orderly manner. The review leader is also responsible for issuing the review report.

The scribe is responsible for documenting findings (for example, defects, inconsistencies, omissions, and ambiguities), decisions, and recommendations made by the review team.

Team members are responsible for their own preparation and for ensuring that the review meets its objectives. Together they are responsible for formulating recommendations in such a way that management can act on them promptly.

4.1.3 When to Hold A Technical Review Meeting

Although the need for conducting technical reviews of specific software elements is defined by project planning documents, additional, unscheduled technical reviews may be conducted at the request of management from various functional areas, according to local procedures. A technical review may not be conducted until the review leader verifies that:

- A statement of objectives for the review is established.
- The responsible individual for the software element indicates readiness for review.
- Specifications for the software element being examined are available.
- Any plans, standards, or guidelines against which the software element are to be examined have been made available.
- The software elements are sufficiently complete for a review to be worthwhile.

Additional reference material can be made available by the individual responsible for the software element, when requested by the review leader.

4.1.4 Procedures

4.1.4.1 Planning The review leader is responsible for the following planning activities:

- Identify the review team.
- Schedule and announce the meeting place.
- Distribute input materials to participants, allowing adequate time for their preparation.

4.1.4.2 Overview A technically qualified person can conduct an overview session for the review team when requested by the review leader. This overview can occur as a part of the review meeting or as a separate meeting.

4.1.4.3 Preparation During the preparation step, each review team member examines the software element and related materials in preparation for the review meeting.

4.1.4.4 Examination At the review meeting, the entire team reviews the software element, evaluating its condition relative to applicable guidelines, specifications, and standards, or evaluates alternative problem solutions. Specifically, the review team examines the software element under review and verifies whether it complies with the specifications and standards. All deviations are recorded.

Additionally, if previously established in the statement of objectives, the team may, for example:

- Document technical issues, related recommendations, and the individual responsible for getting the issues resolved.
- Identify any other issues that must be addressed.

When deficiencies are sufficiently critical or numerous, the review leader can recommend that an additional review process (that is, management review, technical review, or walkthrough) be applied to the reworked software element(s) after the deficiencies have been resolved. This, at a minimum, covers areas changed to resolve deficiencies.

4.1.5 Output

After the software element has been reviewed, a report is generated to document the meeting, listing deficiencies found in the software element. Additionally, if previously established in the statement of objectives, the team may, for example document other findings and describe any recommendations for management. The Technical Review Report identifies:

- The review team members
- The software element(s) reviewed
- Specific inputs to the review
- Unresolved deficiencies in the software element
- Any other findings, as consistent with the statement of objectives (for example, a list of management issues, action item ownership and status, or any recommendations on how to dispose of unresolved issues and deficiencies)

4.2 THE SOFTWARE INSPECTION

4.2.1 Objective

The software inspection process has much in common with the general technical review process. It, too, is used to evaluate a specific software element and provide evidence that the software element satisfies its specifications and conforms to applicable standards. Its statement of objectives includes software element specific objectives. They exist in the form of a checklist that varies with the product being inspected.

Distinctions from the more general technical review process, however, are established by unique V&V objectives. The following always appear in the statement of objectives for the application of the inspection process:

- Detect, identify, and describe software element defects.
- Collect software engineering data (for example, defect and effort data).
- Verify the software element's "fitness for use" in subsequent efforts.
- Ignore alternatives or stylistic issues.
- Provide a delegated control mechanism that determines the next process step.

Moreover, software inspections are typically performed by three to six peer participants led by a moderator impartial to the work product being examined. The moderator is not the author. Defect resolution is mandatory, and rework verification is formal. Both inspection process and product information is recorded.

4.2.2 People and Their Agendas

Roles for the software inspection are similar to those for the technical review, but with the following important distinctions.

All team members, including those with any of the following special responsibilities, are inspectors. The role of inspector is to identify and describe defects in the software element. Inspectors must be knowledgeable of the inspection process. They are chosen to represent different viewpoints at the meeting (for example, requirements, design, code, test, independent test, project management, or quality management). Only those viewpoints pertinent to the inspection of the element are present. The foremost agenda item is defect identification and description.

The review leader is called a *moderator* and the distinction is important because the individual must be *trained* in moderating the inspection process to take full advantage of the synergy available in a small peer review. Because this is a peer review, the moderator is neither significantly higher in rank than the other participants nor closely associated with the software element being inspected. This moderator is the chief planner and meeting manager for the inspection process and is responsible for issuing the inspection reports. The moderator may also be the scribe, but never the author. It is highly recommended that these individuals be trained in the inspection process and interpersonal effectiveness. Training program costs often keep an organization from offering these classes to all possible inspection participants, but it really is critical for the moderators to attend (or to have moderators chosen from those who have attended) classes covering the inspection process. Consistency of inspection process application across the project depends on consistent and capable inspection management. The moderator is "keeper of the process."

A formal role of *reader* has been added so that one person, not many, can present materials. This helps focus attention and control the speed of the inspection. The reader leads the team through its examination of the work product at the inspection meeting. Generally, this is done by paraphrasing sections of the work and by reading line-by-line where required by local standards. Because synergy is the key to inspection success, it is recommended that the reader **not** merely call out: "Are there any problems with 'page 1?' Are there any problems with 'page 2?' . . . " The examination should be more tightly focused than that. Remember that, through focused examination and team member interaction, the team can identify more defects together than the sum total of what they might find individually. Moreover, the inspection rate is important. The reader must proceed quickly enough to keep the attention level of participants while allowing the scribe adequate time to get that job done. The reader is "keeper of the focus and pace."

The role of *scribe* is essentially unchanged from the role found in the technical review, with the exception that standard forms are now required in place of minutes or reports in prose. The scribe documents the defects detected at the meeting and records the product and inspection process data required to fully characterize this particular application of the inspection process. Clarity of written expression and handwriting is important. Typically, forms are used as required by local standards. The scribe is "preserver of knowledge." For meetings with a quick pace, some teams have chosen to have a recorder's assistant who documents every other defect. This allows for a faster pace without hurrying the recorders to the point where their participation drops or defect descriptions suffer.

The *authors* are responsible for meeting inspection entry criteria and for contributing to the inspection based on their special understanding of their own work. They are obligated to perform any rework required to make the work product meet its inspection exit criteria. The author may not serve as moderator, reader, or scribe.

4.2.3 When to Hold the Inspection Meeting

Inspections are planned for, and executed as required for the project and communicated through planning documents, contracts, or local standards. The Software Inspection process can be triggered by:

- Work product availability
- Project plan or schedule compliance
- An inspection outcome that requires a reinspection
- A request from management from any of the various functional areas

One critical distinction from the technical review process is that before setting a date for the inspection meeting, the *moderator verifies* that:

- The software element(s) is available and conforms to project standards for content and format.
- The approved specification for the software element(s) is available.
- All prior milestones are satisfied, as identified in the appropriate planning documents.
- All required supporting documentation is available.
- Any standards guidelines and checklists against which the software element is to be inspected are available, as are all necessary inspection reporting forms.
- For a reinspection, all items noted on the Defect List must have been addressed and that the list is available.

4.2.4 Procedures

4.2.4.1 Planning   During the planning step, the author assembles the inspection package materials for the moderator. The moderator is responsible for ensuring that the materials meet the inspection entry criteria. The moderator is also responsible for ensuring the selection of the inspection team and the assignment of their inspection meeting roles, for scheduling the inspection meetings, and for the distribution of the inspection materials.

4.2.4.2 Overview
If scheduled, an overview presentation of the software element(s) to be inspected is conducted by the moderator, with the author making the presentation. This overview is used to educate the other inspectors concerning the software element and may also be attended by other project personnel who could profit from the presentation.

4.2.4.3 Preparation
It is the individual responsibility of all inspectors to become thoroughly familiar with the software element, using the inspection checklist, the information provided in the overview, and the software specification.

4.2.4.4 Examination
The inspection meeting should follow this agenda:

- Introduce participants and verify preparedness.
- Read software and record defects.
- Review defect list.
- Make exit decision.

To start the meeting, the moderator introduces the participants and describes their roles. The moderator states the purpose of the inspection and directs the inspectors to focus their efforts toward defect detection, not solution-hunting. The moderator reminds the inspectors to direct their remarks to the reader and to comment only on the product, not the author. It may also be useful to resolve any special procedural questions raised by the inspectors. The moderator asks for individual preparation times and records the total on the inspection report. It is the moderator's responsibility to reschedule the meeting if the inspectors are not adequately prepared. The moderator reviews the inspection checklist with the team to ensure that the product has been adequately studied before the inspection meeting.

The reader presents the materials to the inspection team. The inspection team examines the software objectively and the moderator focuses this part of the meeting on creating the defect list. The scribe enters each defect, location, description, and classification on the defect list. During this time, the author answers any specific questions and contributes to defect detection based on his or her special understanding of the software element.

At the end of the inspection meeting, the moderator must have reviewed the defect list with the team to ensure its completeness and accuracy.

The purpose of the exit decision is to bring an unambiguous closure to the inspection meeting. The exit decision determines if the materials meet the inspection exit criteria and prescribes any appropriate rework verification. Specifically, the inspection team identifies the software element disposition as one of the following:

1. Accept: The software element is accepted "as is" or with only minor rework (for example, that would require no further verification).
2. Verify Rework: The software element is to be accepted after the moderator verifies rework.

3. Reinspect: Schedule a reinspection to reexamine the software element after rework completion has been verified by the moderator. At a minimum, this reinspection examines the product areas changed to resolve defects identified in the last inspection.

4.2.5 Output

Typical inspection reports may include a profile of the inspection, some summary of defects found, and a list of those defects.

The inspection profile would contain:

- The number of participants
- The inspection meeting duration
- The size of the materials inspected
- The total preparation time of the inspection team
- The disposition of the software element
- An estimate of the rework effort and rework completion date

The inspection defect summary would show the number of defects identified in each defect category. The defect list would identify each defect, the defect location, description, and category.

4.3 THE WALKTHROUGH

4.3.1 Objective

Although long associated with code examinations, this process is also applicable to other software elements (for example, interface specifications, detailed designs, test specifications or procedures, and change control procedures).

The walkthrough process has much in common with both the general technical review process and the inspection process. It, too, is used to evaluate a specific software element and provide evidence that the software element satisfies its specifications and conforms to applicable standards. Its statement of objectives includes software element specific objectives. They also exist in the form of a checklist that varies with the product being presented. Objectives typically do not pertain to any additional constraints on the walkthrough process.

Distinctions from the other two review processes, however, are established by unique objectives. The following always appear in the statement of objectives for the application of the walkthrough process:

- Detect, identify, and describe software element defects.
- Examine alternatives and stylistic issues.

- Provide a mechanism that enables the authors to collect valuable feedback on their work, yet allows them to retain the decision-making authority for any changes.

Moreover, although a walkthrough team is typically small (that is, as large or smaller than the inspection's three to six participants), objectives have the walkthrough led by the author. This is another significant distinction.

Other important objectives of the walkthrough process include exchange of techniques and style variations, and education of the participants. A walkthrough may point out efficiency and readability problems in the code, modularity problems in design, or untestable design specifications.

4.3.2 People and Their Agendas

Roles for the walkthrough are similar to those for the other two review processes, with one important distinction. The leader responsible for conducting a specific walkthrough, handling the administrative tasks pertaining to the walkthrough, and ensuring that the walkthrough is conducted in an orderly manner is usually the author.

Again, the scribe is responsible for writing down all comments made during the walkthrough that pertain to errors found, questions of style, omissions, contradictions, suggestions for improvement, or alternative approaches.

Each team member is responsible for reviewing any input material prior to the walkthrough and participating during the walkthrough to ensure that it meets its objective. Roles may be shared among the walkthrough members.

4.3.3 When to Hold the Walkthrough Meeting

The need for conducting walkthroughs, as with all product reviews, can be established either by local practice or in planning documents. Completion of a specific software element can trigger the walkthrough for that element. Additional walkthroughs can be conducted during development of the software element at the request of the author or management from various functional areas. A walkthrough is conducted when the author indicates readiness.

4.3.4 Procedures

4.3.4.1 Planning During the planning phase the author:

- Identifies the walkthrough team
- Schedules the meeting and selects the meeting place
- Distributes all necessary input materials to the participants, allowing for adequate preparation time

4.3.4.2 Overview
An overview presentation is made by the author as part of the walkthrough meeting. Before that meeting, however, individual preparation is still required.

4.3.4.3 Preparation
During the preparation phase participants review the input material that was distributed to them and prepare a list of questions and issues to be brought up during the walkthrough.

4.3.4.4 Examination
During the walkthrough meeting:

- The author makes an overview presentation of the software element.
- The author "walks through" the specific software element so that members of the walkthrough team may ask questions or raise issues about the software element, and/or make notes documenting their concerns.
- The scribe writes down comments and decisions for inclusion in the walkthrough report.

At the completion of the walkthrough, the walkthrough team may recommend a follow-up walkthrough. It would follow the same process and would, at a minimum, cover areas changed by the author. The walkthrough process is complete when the entire software element has been walked through in detail and all deficiencies, omissions, efficiency issues, and suggestions for improvement have been noted. The walkthrough report is issued, as required by local standards.

4.3.5 Output

The walkthrough report contains:

- Identification of the walkthrough team.
- Identification of the software element(s) being examined.
- The statement of objectives that were to be handled during this walkthrough meeting.
- A list of the noted deficiencies, omissions, contradictions, and suggestions for improvement.
- Any recommendations made by the walkthrough team on how to dispose of deficiencies and unresolved issues. If follow-up walkthroughs are suggested, that should be mentioned in the report as well.

4.4 IMPLEMENTATION CHALLENGE

Clearly, the goal is to have an economic and effective blend of uniquely repeatable review processes. Each process has characteristic advantages and limitations, and the challenge is to keep each process unique, its execution consistent, and its application part of a well planned (and continuously improving) program of verification and validation. Considerations in meeting this challenge include:

- Application Opportunities: understanding what needs to be reviewed
- Process Mix Planning: knowing the best way to apply the processes
- Multiple Examinations: exercising the option to apply more than one review process (that is, more than one set of objectives) to a given product
- Acceptance and Participation: making human factors work in favor of success
- Execution Consistency: setting the framework for predictability and improvement
- Feedback: providing information to improve the product and the process

4.4.1 Application Opportunities

4.4.1.1 Software Planning Documented plans can also be considered products and examined using the processes detailed in this chapter. The hierarchy of activities addressed by the planning effort, however, often bear little resemblance to the overall structure of the planning documents required on a project. Indeed, the situation across projects and companies varies from having poor plans poorly documented to the less prevalent case where the network of plans provides a true cover for control requirements. All too often, those who have "found religion" after suffering the results of poor planning have gone on to over-document subsequent poor planning efforts. There are myriad plans suggested in the literature, yet little guidance exists to point out interdependencies, overlaps, and possible holes.

For example, a distinction that is subtle to some people is that a project plan and a development plan are two different things. A project plan covers planning considerations for procurement or development, but goes on to address much more. Another problem is that it is often unclear whether a specific plan is more appropriate at the program or project level (recall definitions in Chapter 1). A standard approach for configuration management or quality management at the program level, for example, makes documenting plans at the project level much easier. In this case, intended conformance need only be declared and exceptions (or extensions) noted. That might well be incorporated into a project plan document.

A good analogy is the work done by the software design description standardization effort [IEEE, 1016] of the Institute for Electrical and Electronics Engineers. The fruits of that effort are described as applicable regardless of document structure.

A hierarchy of integrated planning documents is suggested for your project that reflects your specific control needs. For this reason, no specific plan review checklists are provided in the appendixes. Rather, you are directed back to checklists at the program and project levels to help you identify your own needs and a structure that makes sense in your environment.

4.4.1.2 Software Products Perhaps the most widely known product reviews are the software requirements review, the preliminary design review, and the critical design review. Although the program of project and product reviews presented in this book would have these reviews focus purely on product issues, they once played a much more prominent and complex role in software development. It has often been the case that these reviews overreached the product issues represented here and additionally covered select project control issues (for example, concerning feasibility, schedule, progress, and effort).

Without a program of project review, select product reviews have to carry as much of the load as possible. Software requirement reviews have addressed issues germane to reaching a concept closure milestone, and preliminary design reviews have assisted in determining the efficacy of development planning and helped mark the attainment of a project definition milestone. Moreover, by emphasizing the review of critical designs, confidence could be achieved that the project definition milestone had indeed been met.

4.4.2 Process Mix Planning

Determining the identification of products to be examined and the process(es) used can improve the effectiveness and efficiency of your product review program. The following are prerequisite to that planning effort:

- Each type of review to be employed is fully specified.
- Administrative procedures are defined to enable the review to be initiated, executed, recorded, and acted on.
- The responsibility is assigned for the planning, specification, administration, and maintenance of the review process.

One approach that can be used to assist in this planning is to consider the application of product reviews as part of an overall verification and validation program. Then, for each project, review and other V&V activities can be planned in concert.

4.4.2.1 Considerations
One example of how planning review process application extends beyond knowledge of products to be reviewed and the review processes available can be found within code and unit test activities. Well within the heart of the development process model, work associated with code and unit test is repeated more times than work anywhere else in the development cycle. For example, one requirements specification will exist at a higher level of abstraction, but way down in the "details" (Figure 4-1) it is not unreasonable to expect 20 to 100 units, each requiring the same attention. Abstraction is inversely related to repetition, and with increased repetition and the involvement of more people, application consistency is a greater challenge. The other controls in place, and your confidence in them, will influence your choice of review processes at the unit level:

- Hand-off package (to integration) requirements
- Use of simulation and automated testing

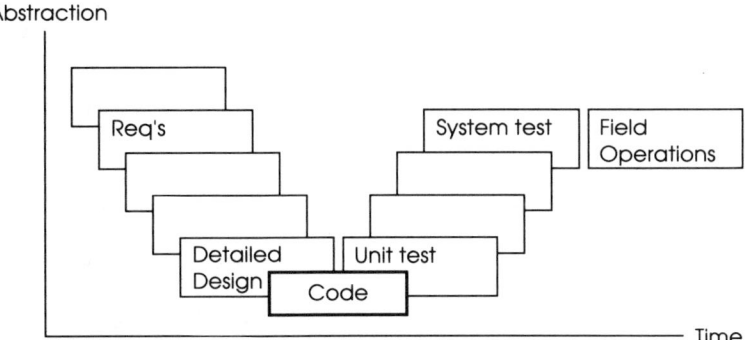

Figure 4-1 Product abstraction versus time

The following factors may also influence your selection:

- Whether the unit represents a new effort or resulted from a fix or enhancement
- The extent of code reuse and the rigor controlling associated libraries
- How critical a specific unit or group of units is to the system
- Whether the same person is responsible for unit design, code, and test

4.4.2.2 Review Process Comparison An example exists, later in this chapter, where multiple examinations can be used in the examination of a specific product. Ruling out that case for now, mapping review processes to products where a single examination step is desired will be studied. Comparing these processes (Figure 4-2), the following guidance can be provided:

- Exposure. If broad exposure and discussion is required, the technical review should be applied.
- Rework. If review team inputs are considered directives rather than advice, inspections should typically be used because rework is required and verified. One possible alternative is the use of the technical review with the added stipulation (that is, stated objective) that rework be verified by the review leader or designee.
- Subject Technology. If the product technology is new or complex, it might be difficult to staff the review team with the appropriate expertise. A technical review or walkthrough might be advisable.
- Subject Volume. If the volume of materials to be reviewed is great, a technical review or walkthrough (depending on required rigor) is advisable. If the materials are easily partitioned, an inspection might still be appropriate.
- Metrics. Data collection requirements may dictate the use of inspections.
- Leadership. The availability of trained moderators is required to support the selection of the inspection process.

	Technical Review	Inspection	Walkthrough
Objective	Established in "Statement of Objectives"	Detect and identify defects. Verify resolution.	Detect defects; examine alternatives; forum for learning
Decision-making	Review team petitions management or technical leadership to act on recommendations	Team chooses from predefined product dispositions. Defects must be removed.	All decisions made by author; change is the prerogative of the author
Change Verification	Leader verifies as part of review report	Moderator verifies rework.	Change verification left to other project controls
The Team	Technical leadership and peer mix; three or more people; leader is usually principal engineer; presenter represents development area and product	College of three to six peers meet with documented attendance; leader is a trained moderator; the presenter is a "reader" other than the author; specific "scribe" duties are identified	Technical leadership and peer mix of two to seven people; leader is usually the author; presenter is usually the author
Material Volume	Moderate to high, depending on the specific meeting "statement of objectives"	Relatively low	Relatively low
Data Collection	Not a formal project requirement; may be done locally	Formally required; defect counts, characteristics, severity, and meeting attributes are kept	Not a formal project requirement; may be done locally

Figure 4-2 Process distinctions for product reviews

- Cost and risk. For critical software, walkthroughs should *not* be used as the sole mechanism.
- History. How long various procedures have been in place may influence process selection (for example, even though inspections might be more appropriate, if new, they might be set aside or only partially used in preference of using walkthroughs if walkthroughs had earlier been established).
- Logistics. The number of process applications for a specific time period and the resources available may influence process selection by directing you toward less rigorous examinations (for example, use the walkthroughs instead of inspections for all but the most critical units).

Other issues to be considered might include:

- Other coverage opportunities for V&V concerns
- The option of applying more than one process

4.4.2.3 The Verification and Validation Plan Whether part of some other project planning document, or as a stand-alone, a Software Verification and Validation Plan (SVVP) [IEEE, 1012] is recommended. This SVVP should, of course, be reviewed to evaluate adequacy of coverage and selection of processes to be applied. Because the plan may be developed incrementally, multiple reviews may be required. Reviews should have participation from all organizational elements governed by the plan. The following concerns need to be addressed by the Software Verification and Validation Plan Review:

- Verification and validation methods (and their completion criteria), as prescribed, ensure requirements traceability for the functional and performance requirements expressed in the software requirements specification.
- The approach, as prescribed, will verify and validate that the product satisfies the requirements of the software requirements specification. The approach should include specific review process applications (for example, technical review, inspection, or walkthrough), demonstration, analysis, and test.
- The approach, as prescribed, requires reports that will adequately document the results of all activities required by the SVVP.
- The approach, as prescribed, brings focus to the definition and control of specific configuration baselines.

In support of these goals, the following may provide a starting point for your SVVP review checklist:

- Identification of V&V tasks, responsibilities, and schedules
- Criteria for evaluating task results
- Identification of prime responsibility for tasks shared by multiple organizational elements
- The requirements for results reporting including reports for task completion, anomaly description, and development process stage completion
- Identification of required resources including staffing, facilities, tools, and budgets
- Identification of special software tools, workbenches, environments, and related training required for the V&V effort
- Identification of any special processes or procedures and related training required for the V&V effort
- Criteria for performing iterating V&V tasks
- Guidance on how to proceed where required inputs do not exist (for example, in certain maintenance efforts)

- Conformance to test documentation standards
- Conformance to review process standards

4.4.3 Multiple Examinations

Using more than one process for a given product can be a great advantage during the development of critical software. The example developed here is for requirements specifications, and is controversial because of the investment involved. It uses walkthroughs early in the specification process to provide a peer examination of the most critical individual requirements, a technical review of the requirements in their entirety, and an inspection of the resulting specification document for fitness for use in subsequent development and test efforts.

4.4.3.1 Motivation
The *IEEE Standard for Software Quality Assurance Plans* [IEEE, 730] says the following about the Software Requirements Review (SRR): "The SRR is held to ensure the adequacy of the requirements stated in the Software Requirements Specification."

The *IEEE Standard for Software Quality Assurance Plans* also defines critical software as "where failure could impact safety or cause large financial or social losses." For critical software, the need for Requirements Specification Examination, however, can go beyond the application of a single process. Although necessary, the popular objectives of completeness, correctness, and feasibility may not be sufficient to ensure predictably high quality in the resulting software. Representation of specifications and the fitness for use of the representation for development, test, and marketing teams could stand additional scrutiny.

Admittedly, no single (and certainly no consensus) approach exists for addressing these issues. The multiprocess requirements examination approach, following shortly, is intended to show one example of how a onetime, single process, requirements examination might be replaced by a mix of distinct examinations of tighter focus. Clearly tied to the most critical of software applications, this approach is not right for all development efforts. However, the reader is asked to recall that the cost of removing a defect in the requirements phase can easily be as little as 0.5 percent of what that same defect might cost you if it were to hit the field.

Although a difference is recognized between a requirement and its form of representation, we will refer to a requirements specification "document," with the knowledge that other representations are possible.

4.4.3.2 Walkthrough of Requirements
Although long associated with code examinations, the walkthrough process is also applicable to software requirements. Indeed, it may be selectively applied to one or more requirements. The major objectives are to find defects (for example, omissions, unwanted additions, and contradictions) in the specification and to consider alternative functionality, performance objectives, or representations. Other important objectives of the walkthrough process include exchange of techniques and style variations, and education of the participants.

In this multiprocess examination approach, this walkthrough process can be used to meet the need for peer approval of individual requirements. It is conducted when the author of the requirements document is ready to present one or more requirements for preliminary evaluation.

4.4.3.3 The Technical Review of Requirements

A technical review can provide a formal team evaluation of software requirement specifications. It identifies any discrepancies from system specifications and standards and/or provides recommendations after the examination of alternatives. This examination may require more than one meeting and typically has a larger attendance than walkthroughs or inspections.

In this multiprocess examination approach, this technical review meets the need for the widespread exposure of requirements to ensure correctness, completeness, and feasibility.

The need for conducting a technical review of software requirements is typically defined by project planning documents. A technical review of requirements is conducted when the author of the requirements specification indicates readiness for review, and the technical review leader is satisfied that the requirements are sufficiently complete for a technical review to be worthwhile.

4.4.3.4 The Inspection of the Specification

We have already seen that the objective of a software inspection is to detect, identify, and describe software element defects. This is a rigorous, though relatively small, peer examination that, for the purpose of this example verifies that the software requirements specification document is fit for use in driving subsequent development and test activities. Specifically, it verifies that:

- The software requirements specification document conforms to applicable standards for format and content.
- The document is not ambiguous.
- Requirements are stated so as to be testable.

The software requirements specification document inspection can be triggered by document availability, schedule compliance, or completion of rework required by an earlier inspection.

Before scheduling the inspection, it is important that:

- Document readiness be verified.
- All required supporting information is available.
- For a reinspection, all required rework has been verified.
- All prior milestones are satisfied, as identified in the appropriate planning documents.

The moderator discusses the inspection checklist with the team to ensure that the product has been adequately studied before the inspection meeting. That checklist should contain elements to ensure that:

58 PRODUCT REVIEWS

- The distribution list identifies the right people, by function.
- The signature/approval block is appropriately designed.
- The document displays the appropriate proprietary markings.
- The document release and issue are clearly designated.
- The table of contents reflects the required structure.
- References are correct and adequate in coverage.
- The "owner" of the post-publication document is identified.
- Any assumptions or dependencies are documented.
- The requirements are clear, unambiguous, and complete.
- Requirement statements are correct and testable, with design appropriately deferred to later stages of development.

4.4.4 Acceptance and Participation

Acceptance is by design rather than by chance. Achieving and maintaining acceptance is the common thread that unifies other concerns. It is accomplished by understanding what motivates the key players and having them participate in identifying, defining, and planning to ensure that their needs are met.

Review program acceptance is needed from the technical staff and their management. The managers are responsible for:

- Training and orientation for the technical staff in the use of the review processes
- Providing the necessary resources of time, personnel, budget, and facilities required to plan, define, execute, and manage the reviews
- Anticipating and supporting product rework
- Reporting review results against project milestone events

In addition, the technical staff is required to exhibit a level of development expertise and product knowledge sufficient to comprehend the software or plan under review. Their buy-in is required to ensure faithful and consistent process execution.

In putting a review program together, the technical staff and their management are your customers and the program's success varies with your ability to gain their acceptance. Attributes common to successful programs (Figure 4-3) should be evident in yours.

Further, toward preserving the commitment of management, periodic reports presenting review results in terms of a return on their investment are necessary. A sample ("Monthly Summary of Product Review Results") is provided in the appendixes.

The technical staff's commitment will be preserved if they see:

- An effort to reduce their difficulties in holding reviews
- Improvement in the products as a result of their participation in reviews
- Their own involvement in improving the review processes and their application

Management	Technical Staff
Educated in verification and validation fundamentals, the available review processes, and in how to mix these processes to meet their V&V needs.	Well informed of review program objectives, and educated in the fundamentals of V&V and in the specifics of the review processes requiring their participation.
Active in defining and approving any measure of the organization's effectiveness or efficiency as related to the review program. Committed to designing any individual performance evaluation *out* of the review program.	Active in defining and any measure of the organization's effectiveness or efficiency as related to the review program. Confident that no instance of proper review process application is used to evaluate individual performance.
Communicative of what decisions need to be made based on review program execution and *what* information is needed to support that decision making.	Communicative of any difficulties in executing review processes, and active in defining and approving *how* data is to be collected.
Reassured that processes are being followed and that they are working.	Committed to faithful process execution.
Committed to rewarding the technical staff for following the process and *not* to penalize for the results of process execution.	Recognized for review participation and rewarded for taking a lead role in process execution and continuous improvement.

Figure 4-3 Ensuring review program acceptance

4.4.5 Execution Consistency

To supply adequate coverage from diverse perspectives, it is suggested that the technical staff contribute in the development of a "required reviewer matrix" (Figure 4-4) for each software element that is to be reviewed. In application, review leaders should reschedule any review where representation is inadequate.

Development process planning is critical to the consistent execution of product reviews. Although not prerequisite for having a successful review program, the following are necessary to document the extent of your program's success or to take full advantage of your review investment:

- Standard entry and exit criteria should be defined for development phases.
- Development standards should provide for consistent product format and content, as well as define any product acceptance criteria.
- The product should be partitioned into manageable, reviewable units.
- The software elements to be reviewed and the review process to be employed should be identified in the project planning documents (for example, Software Quality Assurance Plan, Software Verification Plan, and Software Project Management Plan).

PRODUCT REVIEWS

	Requirements	Arch. design	Detailed design	Code	Hand-off package	System test plan	Feature test plan	Trial plan
Customer Rep	√							√
Systems Engineer	√	√				√		
Design Engineer	√	√	√				√	
Detail Designer		√	√	√	√			
Unit Encoder/Tester			√	√	√			
Support/Field Trial Specialist	√	√				√		√
Systems Integrator		√			√			
Feature Test Engineer		√				√	√	√
System Test Engineer	√	√				√	√	√
Quality Engineer	√					√		√

Figure 4-4 Sample required reviewer matrix

- Support should be provided to the technical staff in the execution of required reviews.

Further discussion on execution support is a good idea because it is perhaps the greatest aid to process execution consistency. If services can be performed to assist the technical staff in setting up for reviews and cleaning up afterwards, acceptance and consistency will both be improved. Moreover, because you have a single team or individual helping to coordinate product reviews, their knowledge can form the basis for tracking overall review progress, improving in-process audit efficiency through sample size determination and scheduling, and in ensuring timely data collection.

The review coordinator, or support team, could:

- Schedule review meetings
- Verify entry criteria
- Solicit required participation
- Duplicate and distribute materials
- Reserve meeting facilities and equipment (for example, overhead or slide projector, flip charts, and conference call bridges)

Another suggestion that can be used separately or in conjunction with central support deals with packaging and delivery of process specific materials (for example, checklists, written procedures, or report forms). In this example, a *review packet* is designed to support process execution and its use is depicted (Figures 4-5 through 4-7). The review packet contains:

- Review Entry Checklist. This is a process checklist used to verify readiness. It is completed by the review leader before announcing the review meeting.
- Meeting Notice. This form identifies the product to be reviewed, its author, where it fits in as a control item, its size, the reason for review, and the review process to be used. Naturally, it also identifies meeting date, time, place, expected duration, team members, and role assignments.
- Role Descriptions. For those requiring a refresher, single-page role descriptions are made available.
- Product Checklist. Unique to each product type, this is the classic checklist and guides product examination.
- Discussion Items List. This form is used to identify and describe problems in the product reviewed and, potentially, possible problems in other products.
- Review Report Form. This form is unique to the review process used, and provides a review summary from a *process* perspective. It identifies the class of product (for example, detailed design specification or product development plan), participants by role and function responsibility (reference the required reviewer matrix, final disposition, and other process data).
- Rework Report Form. This form documents the producer's rework time and the verification time provided by the review leader. In addition, it identifies any items that remain open after rework verification. It is completed by the review leader to document rework verification.

Although these forms are presented as being photocopied and distributed, with some adjustment they could be offered on-line with electronic transmission.

Initial form acceptance is best where the technical universe participated in their design. As with all forms used by the technical universe, a feedback mechanism should exist so their input can be used to evolve the forms and the underlying process.

4.4.6 Feedback

A program of data analysis and in-process auditing is recommended to provide continuous improvement in how your process mix is deployed.

The examinations processes outlined in this chapter can provide data for the analysis of the quality of the software deliverables. Further, they can provide information leading to the improved effectiveness of procedures and evaluation process efficiency. For example, with respect to the inspection process, common practice would suggest up to 1.5 hours preparation, up to 2 hours meeting time, and whatever volume might be comfortably handled in that period of time. The frequency and types of the inspection analysis reports, and their distribution, can also be determined from further studies. To enable these analyses, defects that are identified at the various evaluation meetings can be categorized by defect type, class, and severity.

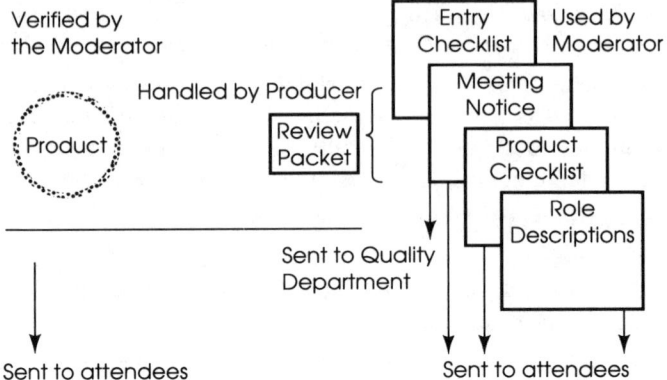

Figure 4-5 Before the review

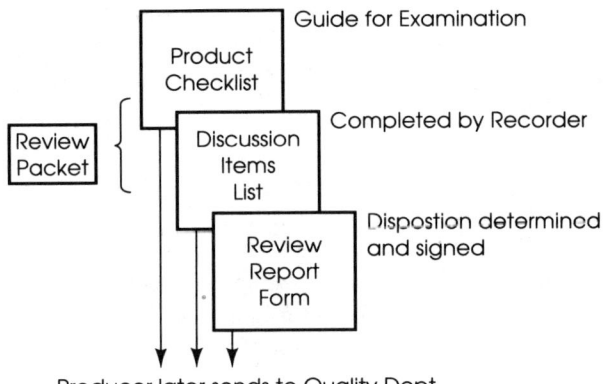

Figure 4-6 During the review

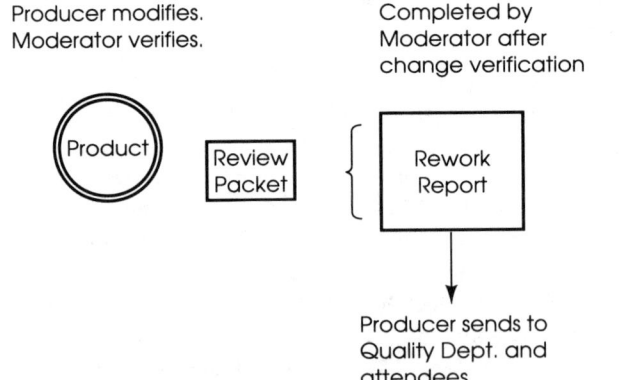

Figure 4-7 After the review

The defect *type* identifies a specific attribute of requirements, and, for example, may be identified as relating to standards compliance, performance, safety, procedure, interface, representation, et cetera.

Defect *class* characterizes evidence of nonconformance, and, for example, may be categorized as "missing," "wrong," or "extra." Additional defect classes used when examining documents could include "ambiguous" or "inconsistent."

Defects are then ranked by *severity*, for example, as "major" for defects that would result in failure of the software element(s) or an observable departure from system specification, or as "minor" for defects that would affect only the nonfunctional aspects of the software element.

In addition to counts of defects by type, class, and severity, retained data could contain the identification and disposition of the product(s) examined, identification of the process used, the date and time of the examination, the name of the review leader, the preparation and meeting times, and the volume of the materials examined.

The management of data requires capabilities for the storage, entry, access, updating, and summary and reporting of the categorized defects. The frequency and types of the analysis reports, and their distribution, are left to the reader.

Once your data collection, analysis, and reporting program is under way, you'll be making process decisions based on the applicability and accuracy of your data. The most prevalent contributor to invalid data is process variance. The consistency of review process application is critical in warding off efficiency deterioration and allowing continuous improvement. You *must* be measuring what you think you are measuring. A program of in-process auditing is recommended to control this problem. Typical program elements include:

- Verify the consistency of the product as it evolves through the development process by determining, on a sampling basis, that hardware and software interfaces are consistent with the Software Requirements Specification (SRS).
- Verify the traceability (and maintenance) of the requirements as the project progresses by determining, on a sampling basis, that the design of the product, as the Software Design Description (SDD) is evolving, satisfies the functional requirements of the SRS.
- Determine compliance with applicable process standards (for example, auditing of the inspection process, on a sampling basis, to determine if inspection process rules are being followed).

You might be surprised at what you learn. For example, if sins of commission are consistently found earlier than sins of omission, auditing could uncover that software requirements are reviewed without a copy of the system requirements available at the meeting. This would explain why missing functionality escapes detection longer than malfunction. Further, if a sudden rash of trouble reports arrive late in the project against the requirements specification document, an audit of review records might indicate that the functions complaining the most were not represented at the examinations. This could have been detected earlier and stopped by using in-process audits.

4.5 SUMMARY

A clear plan regarding product reviews, usually part of the program-level quality plan, needs to be published and widely read. It should identify specific review processes available for use and all products requiring review. The mapping of processes against products may be delegated to project-level plans, but wherever it appears, it should be clear and have process objectives well documented.

Procedurally, the selected review applications must fit well into the overall project methodology and adequately cover any verification and validation concerns delegated to the reviews. Participation and acceptance come more quickly when participants have been well trained and, wherever possible, have contributed to the definition and review of process standards and implementation details.

The challenge is to keep each process unique, its execution consistent, and its application part of a well planned (and continuously improving) program of verification and validation. Considerations in meeting this challenge include managing application opportunities, process mix planning, taking advantage of any opportunities for multiple examinations, encouraging acceptance and participation, ensuring execution consistency, and proving a mechanism for feedback to improve the product and the process.

CHAPTER 5
Audits

The objective of software auditing is to provide an objective compliance confirmation of products and processes to certify adherence to standards, guidelines, specifications, and procedures.

The results of the audit are documented and are typically submitted to the management of the audited organization, to the entity initiating the audit, and to any external organizations identified in the audit plan. The report includes a list of the items in noncompliance or other issues for subsequent review and action. When stipulated by the audit plan, recommendations are reported in addition to the audit results.

This chapter provides a generic process description for auditing and presents specific applications of that process. Program challenges are discussed.

5.1 THE AUDIT PROCESS

5.1.1 Objective

Audits, performed in accordance with documented plans and procedures, provide an independent confirmation that product development and process execution adhere to standards, guidelines, specifications, and procedures. Audit personnel use objective audit criteria (for example, contracts and plans; standards, practices and conventions; or requirements and specifications) to evaluate:

- Software elements
- The processes for producing them
- Projects
- Entire quality programs

5.1.2 People and Their Agendas

It is the responsibility of the audit team leader to organize and direct the audit and to coordinate the preparation and issuance of the audit report. The audit team leader is ultimately responsible for the proper conduct of the audit and its reports, and makes sure that the audit team is prepared.

The entity initiating the audit is responsible for authorizing the audit. Management of the auditing organization assumes responsibility for the audit and the allocation of the necessary resources to perform the audit.

Those whose products and processes are being audited provide all relevant materials and resources and correct or resolve deficiencies cited by the audit team.

5.1.3 When to Audit

The need for an audit is established by one of the following events:

- A special project milestone, calendar date, or other criterion has been met and, as part of its charter, the auditing organization is to respond by initiating an audit.
- A special project milestone has been reached. The audit is initiated per earlier plans (for example, the Software Quality Assurance Plan, or Software Development Plan). This includes planned milestones for controlling supplier development.
- External parties (for example, regulatory agencies or end users) require an audit at a specific calendar date or project milestone. This may be in fulfillment of a contract requirement or as a prerequisite to contractual agreement.
- A local organizational element(s) (for example, project management, functional management, systems engineering, or internal quality assurance/control) has requested the audit, establishing a clear and specific need.

Perhaps the most important inputs required to assure the success of the audit are the purpose and scope of the audit. Observations and evaluations performed as part of the audit require objective audit criteria, such as contracts requirements, plans, specifications, procedures, guidelines, and standards. The software elements and processes to be audited need to be made accessible, as do any pertinent histories. Background information about the organization responsible for the products and processes being audited (for example, organization charts) are critical for both planning and execution of the audit.

5.1.4 Procedures

The auditing organization develops and documents an audit plan for each audit. This plan should, in addition to restating the audit scope, identify the:

- Project processes to be examined (provided as input) and the time frame for audit team observation.

- Software to be examined (provided as input) and their availability. Where sampling is used, a statistically valid sampling methodology is used to establish selection criteria and sample size.
- Reporting requirements (that is, results report, and optionally, the recommendations report with their general format and distribution defined). Whether recommendations are required or excluded should be explicitly stated.
- Required follow-up activities.
- Activities, elements, and procedures necessary to meet the scope of the audit.
- Objective Audit Criteria that provide the basis for determining compliance (provided as input).
- Audit Procedures and Checklists.
- Audit Personnel requirements (for example, number, skills, experience, and responsibilities).
- Organizations involved in the audit (for example, the organization whose products and processes are being audited).
- Date, time, place, agenda, and intended audience of "overview" session (optional).

The audit team leader prepares an audit team having the necessary background and (when allowed) notifies the involved organizations, giving them a reasonable amount of advance warning before the audit is performed. The notification should be written to include audit scope, the identification of processes and products to be audited, and the auditors' identity.

An optional overview meeting with the audited organization is recommended to "kick-off" the examination phase of the audit. The overview meeting, led by the audit team leader, provides:

- Overview of existing agreements (for example, audit scope, plan, and related contracts)
- Overview of production and processes being audited
- Overview of the audit process, its objectives, and outputs
- Expected contributions of the audited organization to the audit process (that is, the number of people to be interviewed, meeting facilities, et cetera)
- Specific audit schedule

The following preparations are required by the audit team:

- Understand the organization: It is essential to identify functions and activities performed by the audited organization and to identify functional responsibility.
- Understand the products and processes: It is a prerequisite for the team to learn about the products and processes being audited through readings and briefing.
- Understand the Objective Audit Criteria: It is important that the audit team become familiar with the objective audit criteria to be used in the audit.

- Prepare for the Audit Report: It is important to choose the administrative reporting mechanism that will be used throughout the audit to develop the report that follows the layout identified in the audit plan.
- Detail the audit plan: Choose appropriate methods for each step in the audit program.

In addition, the audit team leader makes the necessary arrangements for:

- Team orientation and training
- Facilities for audit interviews
- Materials, documents, and tools required by the audit procedures
- The software elements to be audited (for example, documents, computer files, personnel to be interviewed)
- Scheduling interviews

Elements that have been selected for audit are evaluated against the Objective Audit Criteria. Evidence is examined to the depth necessary to determine if these elements comply with specified criteria

The audit should, as appropriate to its scope:

- Review procedures and instructions.
- Examine work breakdown structures.
- Examine evidence of implementation and balanced controls.
- Interview personnel to ascertain the status and functioning of the processes and the status of the products.
- Examine element documents.
- Test the element(s).

An audit is considered complete when:

- Each element(s) within the scope of the audit has been examined.
- Findings have been presented to the audited organization.
- Response to draft findings have been received and evaluated.
- Final findings have been formally presented to the audited organization and initiating entity.
- The audit report has been prepared and submitted to recipients designated in the audit plan.
- The recommendation report, if required by plan, has been prepared and submitted to recipients designated in the audit plan.
- All of the auditing organization's follow-up actions included in the scope (or contract) of the audit have been performed.

5.1.5 Output

Following a standard framework for audit reports, the draft and final audit reports contain:

- Audit Identification: Report title, audited organization, auditing organization, and date of the audit.
- Scope: Scope of the audit, including an enumeration of the standards, specifications, practices, and procedures constituting the Objective Audit Criteria against which the audit of the software elements and processes was conducted.
- Conclusions: A summary and interpretation of the audit findings, including the key items of non-conformance.
- Synopsis: A listing of all the audited software elements and processes, and associated findings.
- Follow-up: The type and timing of audit follow-up activities.

Additionally, when stipulated by the audit plan, recommendations are provided to the audited organization, or the entity that initiated the audit. Recommendations are reported separately from results.

Comments and issues raised by the audited organization must be resolved. The final audit report should then be prepared, approved, and issued by the audit team leader to the organizations specified in the audit plan.

5.2 SPECIFIC PROCESS APPLICATIONS

5.2.1 The Software Quality Program Audit

In general, the purpose of a Software Quality Program Audit (SQPA) is to establish:

- How well the current quality program documentation addresses the basic elements of sound practice as required by the company and as recognized in industry
- How well that organization follows its formal program

The SQPA is sometimes known as a Quality Program Evaluation (QPE) or Quality System Audit (QSA), although it is preferable to think of QPEs and QSAs as being much broader in scope than covering only the software quality program. An SQPA in this sense would represent an activity set that could be performed as part of the more extensive QPE or QSA. Sample letters, plans, and reports in the appendixes can be tailored to meet your own SQPA program needs. They can also be edited to provide coverage for other auditing needs.

During the course of an SQPA, the audit team works very closely with management and personnel to manage audit team interactions with the organization and to minimize interference with their regular activities. Five general methods of information gathering are used to characterize the quality program.

- Examination of process documentation
- Examination of selected in-process products
- Interview of staff
- Process witnessing
- Case study

Key Audit contacts within the audited organization will be informed regularly of audit progress. Moreover, these contacts will regularly desk check the results report as it is being developed and will participate in a formal review of the final draft. Their participation in verifying report accuracy is critical to audit success.

Quality program documentation will be examined for coverage, consistency and uniformity of purpose, and adequacy. The audit team will request specific documentation on initiating the audit. All documents considered in the program documentation analysis will be identified in the results report. The audit team may request sample in-process documentation representative of work in the area or specific documents in their examination of quality program execution.

It is recommended that each interview last approximately 30 minutes. The appropriate interview candidates will be identified by the key contacts and selected by the audit team. Handouts should be made available so that interviewees will know what to expect.

The audit team should be notified of all project-level meetings planned for the audit period. Also, the audit team should be afforded an opportunity to witness any activities identified in the plan for the specific audit effort. Their attendance at meetings, tour of facilities, and witnessing of specific project activities is an important part of determining how the quality program is executed.

As part of the audit process, a recently released product or process can have its history reviewed along with the current perception of overall quality. This is typically the case where the documented results of other audits are available (for example, in-process audits, functional configuration audits, and physical configuration audits). Subsequent to the audit examination, the audit team will issue a draft audit report to the audited organization for review and comments.

Audit team rework of the audit report occurs before formal results reporting. This rework is performed in concert with the draft report review to resolve any misunderstandings or ambiguities while maintaining objectivity and correctness. It also serves to ensure report usability by adding consistency to the level of report details and by adding any freshly verified information. The recommended practice is to involve representatives of the audited organization in reviewing audit results, as:

1. An ongoing, periodic activity integrated into the overall examination schedule, or
2. A closure step to the examination period.

Involving the audited organization contributes to report quality through interaction and the possible delivery of any further evidence.

The audit team should conduct a post-audit conference to review with audited organization staff the deficiencies, findings, and (if applicable) recommendations. Comments and issues raised by the audited organization must be resolved.

The final audit report (for example, executive summary) should then be prepared, approved, and issued by the audit team leader to the organizations specified by the audit plan.

5.2.2 The In-process Audit

In-process audits are held any time prior to the completion of system testing (that is, typically before the functional audit to be described later) to verify the consistency of the design and proper process execution. These audits follow the general audit process description and are applied any, or all, of three ways according to local standards:

- Examine all elements of a product class (for example, all requirements specifications) or all applications of a specific process (for example, all inspections).
- Examine a statistical sample of a product class (for example, a percentage of detailed designs) or a statistical sample of a specific process (for example, a percentage of inspections).
- Examine specific, critical elements of a product class (e.g., the interface specification for the XXX subsystem) or specific, critical process applications (for example, requirements reviews).

Although the scope may vary, the general approach holds. In-process audit procedures are unique to the process and product examined. Specific procedures should be established locally using the general steps found in Section 5.1.

The results report for in-process audits should identify all discrepancies found and prove an overall opinion. The opinion should take the form of approval, contingent approval, or disapproval. Because in-process audits are frequently performed on behalf of project management as prerequisite to meeting a project milestone, significant compliance deviations must be corrected or waived by project management. This cycle should complete during or before the functional configuration audit.

5.2.2.1 Example Product Consistency Audit In-process audits can be applied to determine the consistency of the product as it evolves through the development process. The example presented here determines, on a sampling basis, that:

- Hardware and software interfaces are consistent with design requirements in the Software Requirements Specification (SRS).

- The code is fully tested by the SVVP to ensure that the functional requirements of the SRS are satisfied.
- The design of the product, as the Software Design Description (SDD) is evolving, satisfies the functional requirements of the SRS.
- The code is consistent with the SDD.
- Requirements are traceable.

5.2.2.2 Example Audit of Process Execution In-process audits can be applied to determine compliance with applicable process standards. The example presented here is auditing the inspection process, on a sampling basis, to determine if inspection process rules are being followed.

Input material should include formal process descriptions and a product sample evidencing process execution.

5.2.3 Configuration Audits

As apposed to in-process audits that tend to occur over a period of time, configuration audits are applied to provide a snapshot in time. That snapshot provides an objective evaluation of whether a configuration baseline (or item) is or is not in agreement with specifications. This agreement must be both functional and physical.

The *IEEE Standard Glossary of Software Engineering Terminology* [IEEE,729] defines Configuration Auditing as:

> The process of verifying that all required configuration items have been produced, that current version agrees with specified requirements, that the technical documentation completely and accurately describes the configuration items, and that all change requests have been resolved.

To eliminate confusion over what is being audited, the audit plan (or contract in project plans) and reports should identify software elements by nomenclature, specification identification number, configuration item number, and brief description.

Typical materials required by the audit team include:

- Standards (for example, nomenclature, labeling, or media control)
- Specifications (for example, functional, performance, interface, architecture, and detailed design specifications)
- Products (for example, source and object code, approved nomenclature, markings, nameplates, software version description, deliverable diagnostics, or deliverable documentation)
- Known problems (for example, current waivers against specific configuration items, the software verification and validation report, in-process audit reports for items under audit, other configuration audit reports)
- Known changes (for example, approved changes identified by state of completion)

- Test information (for example, the plans, specifications, procedures, reports, identification of all successfully accomplished and unexecuted functional testing, and the status of test programs to test configured items with automatic test equipment)
- Delivery information (for example, packaging plan or installation plan)

Whenever differences exist between the configuration of the system in the development environment and the specific configuration of the system under examination, they must be noted and evaluated. It is critical to certify or otherwise demonstrate that differences do not degrade the functional or performance characteristics of the system or impede the test organization's ability to evaluate the system.

The audit team should examine the system for vendor-provided or supplier-developed software, and seek evidence that any such software elements were produced under reasonable and prudent quality controls.

The examples of the physical configuration audit and the functional configuration audit have been chosen for a more detailed look at activities typical to configuration auditing.

5.2.3.1 The Physical Configuration Audit The physical configuration audit provides an independent evaluation of whether components in the "as-built version" map to its specifications. Specifically, "this audit is held to verify that the software and its documentation are internally consistent and are ready for delivery" [IEEE, 730]. Activities typically planned and executed as part of a physical configuration audit include evaluations of:

- Product composition and structure
- Product functionality
- Change controls

The audit team should examine the documented baseline and identify the composition of any configuration in terms of its subordinate units. The physical existence of the configuration is then compared to this documented baseline and standards for markings, nomenclature, packaging, and so on. Functionality is usually determined through examination of the functional configuration audit.

The audit team should verify that the change control system can identify and describe the parent element of a given configuration item by unit identifier. Further, the system must in a broader sense be able to describe the composition of any configuration item or its identifier with respect to other configuration items or identifiers. It must also, in support of change control, be able to identify related specifications and outstanding changes given a specific identifier.

The audit report should include an evaluation within the standard audit report framework. The evaluation should take the form of:

Approval: The system of software elements has been observed as having all deliverable components accounted for and as being of compatible issue.

Contingent Approval: The evaluation of the system of software elements results in approval given successful completion of specific, well-defined (observable) corrective action.

Disapproval: The system of software elements was observed to be seriously inadequate.

5.2.3.2 The Functional Configuration Audit

The functional configuration audit provides an independent evaluation of configuration items to determine whether actual functionality and performance are consistent with the requirement specifications. Specifically, "this audit is held prior to the software delivery to verify that all requirements specified in the Software Requirements Specification have been met" [IEEE, 730].

Activities typically planned and executed as part of a functional configuration audit include:

- Evaluation of earlier verification and validation efforts
- Testing of the product
- Evaluation of the test approach and results attained
- Tracing requirements from their initial specification through system level testing
- Evaluating the consistency between baselined product elements

An examination of the software verification and validation report to establish it's accuracy is usually one of the first things done. All problem reporting and corrective action is reviewed to confirm that problems have been adequately reported and that changes have been approved, are technically correct, and have been properly incorporated and verified.

Responsibility for testing varies across the industry. Acceptable scenarios here include cases where:

- Testing is performed by an independent test organization under the scrutiny of the audit team.
- Testing is performed through a partnership of the independent test organization and the audit team.
- Testing is performed by the audit team.

Regardless of the approach taken, the audit team provides an evaluation of the test approach and results attained. This includes an examination of the formal test documentation against test data. Results are checked for completeness and accuracy, and deficiencies are documented.

Requirements are traced from their initial specification through system-level testing. The examination of test matrices is an important part of this effort. Typically as a sample, code is compared with its documented specifications to establish whether the code addresses its documented requirements. Equally important is whether the code provides any unspecified functionality.

Toward evaluating the consistency between baselined product elements, design review outputs are sampled to confirm whether all findings have been incorporated and completed. Driven by this sampling, updates to previously delivered documents are reviewed for accuracy and consistency.

This audit is concerned not only with functionality, but also with performance. Configuration item performance should be established by having accomplished testing with appropriate test documentation and validated data. For performance parameters that cannot be verified completely during testing, simulations or other analysis should be performed. The audit should establish the level of confidence that the configuration item will perform, in regular operation, as stated in its specifications and performance criteria.

The audit report should include an evaluation within the standard audit report framework. The evaluation should take the form of:

Approval: The software element(s) has been observed as having all required functions and shows evidence of meeting minimum performance standards.

Contingent Approval: The evaluation of the software element(s) would result in approval given successful completion of specific, well-defined (observable) corrective action.

Disapproval: The software element(s) were observed to be seriously inadequate.

5.3 IMPLEMENTATION CHALLENGE

The objective of software auditing is to provide an objective evaluation of products and processes to confirm compliance to standards, guidelines, specifications, and procedures. The following are prerequisite to achieve that objective:

- Objective audit criteria exist (for example, contracts, requirements, plans, specifications, standards) against which software elements and processes can be evaluated.
- Audit personnel are selected to promote team objectivity. They are usually independent of any direct responsibility for the products and processes examined and may be from an external organization.
- Audit personnel are given sufficient authority by appropriate management to perform the audit.

5.3.1 The Challenge of Auditing

As a prerequisite to audit success, we have the following issues:

1. Cooperation of the organization(s) being audited
2. The integrity of the audit process

3. Auditor skill and knowledge base
4. The extent of positive post-audit change or increased confidence

Although issues 2 through 4 are handled extensively by this handbook, perhaps the best place to start is with challenges encountered at the initiation of a typical audit: Issue 1, the cooperation of the organization being audited.

The point here is simple: The needed cooperation can only come from organizational and personal commitment to the audit process. People will only make a commitment if they understand what is happening, and believe it will be a positive contribution toward meeting their perceived needs. The general attitude toward the audit is based on these two commitment factors.

A common understanding (or the lack thereof) is affected by, but not limited to their organizational and personal past experiences with audit activities. In fact, you may uncover (or freely be offered) the following beliefs:

- Audits uncover insignificant problems and fail to address real issues.
- Auditors are like bulls. They run around in a frantic rage that interrupts your operations, graze in your pastures, and leave behind their trademark.

Even when a common understanding of audit scope, objectives, and procedures exists, communication and judgment barriers can act as sources for errors that may detract from the audit's real usefulness. Examples include:

- Phraseology
- Semantic equivalence
- Identification
- Interview momentum
- Relying on the "mean"
- Auditing process maturity
- The ability to act on recommendations
- Product maturity

You get what you ask for, so avoid question phrasing that is either slanted, biased, or incriminating (for example, "You don't think X, do you?"; "What do you think of those idiots?"; and "Do you still beat your dog?" respectively).

Some words (and most acronyms) can have multiple meanings. This can influence how well a question or its answer is understood. Moreover, "intellectual" words or words not in common use are not only frequently misunderstood, but create a natural hesitation by listeners to admit that the word is not understood.

We all have predetermined opinions of ourselves, others, and certain philosophies and objects. In fact, it is common to identify with a specific person or set of beliefs. Automatic answers tend to reflect these sets rather than reality. Be reluctant to accept a characteristic as "common," unless local evidence supports that conclusion.

There is an unwanted, though common, tendency to let first impressions of the interviewee distort hearing. Specifically, a tendency exists to over-rate earlier answers where a good first impression was made. Similarly, good answers may, inappropriately, be discounted owing to earlier poor responses. First impressions must be controlled.

Where the equivalent question is presented to several people, there may be a tendency for the auditor to accept the common response as representing reality. This is a departure from sound auditing principles. Avoid this situation by formalizing your impression, as based on the mean response, and seek verification through further questioning. Consensus and reality are not synonymous.

Auditing process maturity really represents the "quality of measurement." Experience at performing audits, auditing skills, and subject matter expertise are some indicators of auditing process maturity.

You must walk before you can run. Keep that saying in mind when constructing recommendations. Keep them do-able. As a related concern, beware of the common misconception that acting on all recommendations will produce a perfect process.

Product maturity, the positioning of the product in its life cycle, is an important issue to consider when constructing recommendations. Given that a recommendation is technically sound and that the organization has the ability to act on that recommendation, the organization must still be able to foresee a return on their investing resources in response to your recommendation. If a product is nearing retirement, long-term investments in process improvement may be unwarranted. An exception to this might be where the process change would further develop skills in individuals targeted for transfer to other projects.

Real value to the audited organization's management team comes from being able to answer questions like the following and to show how they can proceed with "do-able" improvement projects in what they consider key areas.

- Are the products fit-for-use?
- Is product quality competitive?
- Are governing policies and procedures being followed?
- Is our process in line with industry and our customers' expectations (or requirements)?
- Are we setting reasonable plans and then following them?
- What are the current roadblocks to product and process quality?
- What roadblocks lie in our strategic direction?

5.3.2 Audit Leadership

The scope of Audit Functions should expand to be consistent with your organization's approach to Total Quality Control (TQC). Moreover, care should be taken to keep the auditing function in line with overall corporate goals. This may require forcing policy statements to be established or the standards base to be strengthened.

People are the key to effectiveness (that is, "Are we doing the right things?") and efficiency (that is, "Are we doing them well?"). Continued audit process improvement should be your goal. The best place to start is probably with improving the communication skills of auditors. People from the entire range of organizations audited should be involved in promoting participative concepts of auditing. Keeping your audit staff multidisciplinary, augmenting your audit team with borrowed subject matter experts from organizations similar to the targeted organization will:

- Increase credibility
- Improve scheduling efficiency
- "Seed" organizations under your influence with Quality Assurance (QA) knowledge

Files should be maintained, identifying potential team members. This should encompass not just your audit professionals, but also the aforementioned subject matter experts. Personal characteristics, formal education, technical training, communication skills, experience, and availability should be tracked.

Once formed, your audit team should be briefed on:

- Audit scope and objectives
- Applicable policies and procedures
- Governing documentation and contract agreements
- Key organizational contacts
- The tentative schedule and travel forecast

Other start-up activities that should be assigned include, but are not limited to the identification or development of checklists and other aids, and accommodations and other arrangements.

It also helps to assign lead responsibility for the results and recommendations reports, documentation analysis, and interviewing.

Some details often overlooked during audit planning include:

- Identifying the possible complexities of local travel and communications
- Meeting arrangement confirmation responsibilities
- Getting any necessary passes for entry and property removal

5.3.3 The Auditor

The auditor is to use sound judgment, based on demonstrable skills and experience, and is expected to remain objective and unbiased. Diplomatically using positive dialogue and written communication skills, the auditor is an agent of positive change. As such, honesty and confidentiality are required.

QA knowledge and technical expertise are the foundation on which effective communication skills allow the construction of a sound relationship with the audited organizations. Skilled in interacting with various personality types and management levels, the effective auditor must be a versatile communicator. Both analysis and synthesis are practiced by the most effective auditors.

Characteristics to be avoided include:

- Opinionated or argumentative
- Feels obligated to find something wrong
- Lacks the discipline to prepare adequately for interviews
- Easy to sidetrack
- Believes without verification
- Would rather speak than listen

As a team, auditors must possess these positive characteristics:

- Training and experience in quality assurance/quality control practices
- Experience in auditing techniques
- Knowledge of statistics
- Technical expertise that relates to the area audited
- Managerial and business knowledge relating to the area audited
- Both analysis and synthesis skills
- Strategic and tactical planning skills
- Love of generalities and macro models
- Love of details and micro models

Each auditor must possess the following positive characteristics:

- Natural curiosity and persistence
- Diplomacy
- Self motivation
- Good communicator
- Objective and unbiased
- Appreciative of the imposition placed on the audited organization

5.3.4 The Seven Sins

Some of the most common (and damaging) errors that an auditor can make are presented in Figure 5-1.

5.4 SUMMARY

A generic process description for auditing has been presented that can be used to provide an objective compliance confirmation of products and processes to certify adherence to standards, guidelines, specifications, and procedures.

The Seven Sins

1. *Image Degradation.* — Specifically, do not: •Forget that your audit is an imposition. •Be negative or condemning. •Drink before interviews. •Be late or miss schedules. •Use profane language. •Start (or allow) any disagreements between team members. •Criticize people's efforts.

2. *Violation of Trust.* — Maintain and guard trust. Do not: •Criticize people in front of their boss or peers. •Discuss others you have audited. •Quote people in your reports.

3. *Credibility Assassination.* — The quickest way to lose credibility is: •Argue. You've asked, and been told. Be quiet. •Ask questions without the background to appreciate the answer.

4. *Intergalactic travel.* — Be neither a "black hole" nor a "supernova." You should not: •Forget to give periodic feedback while the audit is in progress. •Project that the audit is "top secret." But, it's also unwise to: •Recommend prematurely. •Talk so much that you forget to listen.

5. *Philosophizing.* — Never, but never: •Be sarcastic. •Discuss personalities. •Get into technical arguments. •"Educate" interviewees.

6. *Discipleship.* — One of the sins most damaging to open communications is committed if you discuss: •Politics. •Religious beliefs. •Company policy (obviously it is OK to quote policy, but never convey that you are in a position to interpret policy.)

7. *Forgotten commitment.* — Do not forget ultimate goals and established agreements. Never: •Distribute reports outside an accepted distribution list. •Use excessive rigor of examination. •Proceed without regard for the imposition on the audit target.

Figure 5-1 The Seven Sins

The need for an audit, whether pertaining to company activities or to supplier controlled development, is established by one of the following events:

- A project milestone has been reached.
- External parties demand an audit at a specific calendar date or project milestone.

- A local organizational element has requested the audit, establishing a clear and specific need.
- A special project milestone, calendar date, or other criterion has been met and, as part of its charter, the auditing organization is to respond by initiating an audit.

Audits, similar in many ways to other examinations, differ in independence and authority. These two examination attributes are closely related. With independence comes absolute authority on the execution of the contracted audit but no authority to mandate any corrective course or plan of action.

Software quality program audits were discussed with the intent of showing how to determine:

- How well the current quality program documentation addresses the basic elements of sound practice as required by the company and as recognized in industry
- How well that organization follows its formal quality program

In-process audits were presented as a way to verify the consistency of designs and proper process execution. These audits follow the general audit process description and are applied any, or all, of three ways according to local standards:

- Examine all elements of a product class.
- Examine a statistical sample of a product class.
- Examine specific, critical elements of a product class.

Although the scope may vary, the general approach holds. In-process audit procedures are unique to the process and product examined. Specific procedures should be established locally.

As opposed to in-process audits, configuration audits are applied to provide a snapshot that provides an objective evaluation of whether a configuration baseline (or item) is, or is not, in agreement with specifications. This agreement must be both functional and physical.

Four conditions were identified as a prerequisite to the success of any of the audits we discussed. First is the required level of cooperation from the organization(s) being audited. Although complete cooperation is not required, some buy-in or acceptance is usually required. Kick-off presentations, general professionalism, and adhering to the rules of conduct presented in this chapter will promote your audit's success. Second, the integrity of the audit process is important. Plan and execute according to plan following a standard audit process and applying objective, and appropriate, audit criteria. A third condition of success is your ability to invest in your auditors to improve their skill and knowledge base. The three conditions, if adequately pursued will contribute to meeting the fourth condition: the extent of positive post-audit change and the increased confidence it brings.

CHAPTER 6

Special Topics

No discussion of reviews and audits would be complete without addressing some of the special topics related to their application.

6.1 INTERVIEWING

6.1.1 Preparation

In preparation for an interview meeting, make sure that all homework has been done. Documents providing background information about the interviewee's group and personal responsibilities and activities should have been read. Answer the question "Why do I want to talk to this individual?" Plan accordingly. Because an interview is a series of interactions meant to reach a specific goal (as you will see in the next section), identify how you will know if the interview is a success. It is best to know, for the worst case (that is, where meeting control is lost), what the single most important question is to ask of the individual. Act according to priorities and do not get lost in philosophy or areas where neither you nor your interviewee have any expertise.

6.1.2 Elements of Success

The following meeting elements are representative of a good interview, but do not necessarily occur in the order shown:

> Introductions. Establish the atmosphere of friendly cooperation.
> Warm up. Allow the interviewee time to settle down, and to know who you are.
> Commitment. Get the interviewee to "buy in" to what you are doing. Establish trust; get the interviewee's cooperation.

Closure. Exit with an expression of appreciation for the interviewee's time and help. Summarize the major points of your understanding and how it was aided. Invite further contact.

Follow up. Remember to thank the interviewee again. Also provide or pick up any additional information you might have promised each other.

6.1.3 Skill Improvement

A very frugal and easy way to improve personal and team interviewing skills is to spend:

1. Five minutes before the interview discussing why each team member wants to interview this person and what would indicate a successful interview. Team interviewing roles should be established (for example, who has the lead for meeting management or who is the principal note taker).
2. Five minutes after the interview to discuss communication flow, meeting management, and potential interview process improvements.

6.1.4 Active Listening

Active listening can be a real challenge. The key point, however, is easy to remember: If you are talking, you are not listening. It is critical that the interviewee feels truly understood. This requires your active participation in the dialogue, not just shooting questions and recording impressions.

- Remove distractions. Do not doodle, walk around, look at the clock or out the window, or shuffle papers.
- Make eye contact with the interviewee and promote the belief that you are paying attention (after all, you should be).
- Do not interrupt or correct the interviewee when the question is being answered. If the pause is too great between question and answer, offer to rephrase or repeat the question. If the interviewee appears uncomfortable, discuss it! Be patient.
- Acknowledge the answer without judgment. Respond to both the answer and any underlying feelings the interviewee may have.
- Remember, there are no "right" answers, only truthful ones. Do not give the impression that you are looking for a specific answer or that the one received is unwanted.
- As a mental exercise, frequently put yourself in your interviewee's position.

6.1.5 Questioning

When verifying someone else's earlier statement, present the question so that the statement will be recognizable if it goes into the report. If you have prepared a checklist, remember that an auditor does not have to ask questions where the answer is obvious from observation or other responses.

Open questions (that is, who, what, when, where, why, and how) should be asked to minimize the risk of biasing the answer or over-directing the question. Directed questions have their place in statement verification, but over-directing can keep the interviewee from volunteering additional information that may be of greater value to the audit.

Do not rely solely on checklists. Remember, if that were appropriate, we would not be needed; a questionnaire could be mailed out! Frequently an auditor has to depart from the prepared checklist to dive deeper into an issue or to verify information gleaned elsewhere. Never use slang, acronyms, or quality assurance (QA) jargon.

Questions that are not neutral invite answers that do not necessarily reflect reality and can trigger unwanted emotions in the interviewee. Moreover, avoid asking closed questions—those that generally receive a "yes/no" answer (for example, those typically starting with is/are, has/have, do/does, can, or will.)

Get the interviewee's answer, not the one that is philosophically or politically correct (or boss induced). If you interview more than one person at a time, it may be wise to separate levels of management to lessen inhibitions and help get full responses.

6.2 REPORT WRITING

The purpose of this section is to provide some guidance on report writing. Getting started appears to be the greatest problem (with the exception, perhaps, of getting your reports read). It is easier to edit than write, so sample letters and reports have been included in the appendixes for your modification and use. To maximize usefulness and improve the internal consistency of this section, the Software Quality Program Audit (SQPA) is referenced wherever documents are discussed, as this audit activity has the broadest scope of those discussed in this book.

6.2.1 Audit Plans

A complete, concise, and well executed plan is crucial to successful audit completion. A successful audit is one where: (1) Results accurately portray the true program state, (2) Recommendations are both possible and appropriate, and (3) Recipients of the report have confidence in the report and a willingness to respond to the recommendations. The audit plan is published by the audit team after review by the audited organization and executive support. Typical milestones would include:

- Key organizational contacts identified, and briefed
- Audit plan approval
- Documentation requested
- Documentation delivered
- Interviews scheduled
- Interviews started

- Documentation analysis complete
- Main interviews completed
- First results report draft issued to key contacts
- Follow-up interviews complete
- Characterization complete
- Results report reviewed, revised, and published
- Recommendations report published
- Executive summary drafted
- Executive summary reviewed, revised, and published
- Response to recommendations received

With the trial-use application of an auditing process, distribution of the report would be limited to the local management team. Specifics will be identified in the audit plan.

6.2.2 Results Report

This is the documented result of having (1) examined current documentation, (2) interviewed selected staff members, and (3) made other project observations. The Results Report will be objective, verifiable, and will contain no recommendations or other subjective expressions of opinion. This report is published by the audit team after review by the audited organization. A typical table of contents for the SQPA Results Report is provided in Figure 6-1.

6.2.3 Recommendations Report

This is the formal presentation of recommendations to management. Recommendations are based on audit results, the business environment, and the past experiences and subjective judgments of the audit team. It is left to the recipients of this report to collaborate in decisions establishing priorities and to chart a course of action. Recommendations are published (and response requested) by the audit team. A typical table of contents for the Recommendations Report from an SQPA is found in Figure 6-2.

Each recommendation presented in this report will consist of:

- Concise statement of recommendation
- Summary of supporting evidence
- Perceived implementation costs and expected benefits
- Risk of no action

For the reader's convenience, all recommendations are restated without their supporting discussions in a special "Summary" section of this report.

Please note that process improvements do not always require increased expenditures and effort. Excessive control and perfectionism are to be avoided as much as inadequate control and unpredictable quality. The audit team's objective is to

1. INTRODUCTION
2. AUDIT SCOPE
3. AUDIT EXECUTION
4. SOFTWARE QUALITY PROGRAM DOCUMENTATION ANALYSIS
    4.1   PURPOSE
    4.2   REFERENCE DOCUMENTS
    4.3   MANAGEMENT
    4.4   DOCUMENTATION
    4.5   STANDARDS, PRACTICES, AND CONVENTIONS
    4.6   REVIEWS AND AUDITS
    4.7   CONFIGURATION MANAGEMENT
    4.8   PROBLEM REPORTING AND CORRECTIVE ACTION
    4.9   TOOLS, TECHNIQUES, AND METHODOLOGIES
    4.10 CODE CONTROL
    4.11 MEDIA CONTROL
    4.12 SUPPLIER CONTROL
    4.13 RECORDS COLLECTION, MAINTENANCE, & RETENTION
5. ANALYSIS OF QUALITY PROGRAM EXECUTION
    5.1   PROCESS MODEL
    5.1.1   Phase 1: | NOTE- Each phase discussion includes:
    5.1.2   Phase 2: | Tasks, responsibilities, deliverables,
    5.1.n   Phase n: | verification and validation, and liaisons
    5.2   PROCESS CONTROLS
    5.2.1   Project Management
    5.2.2   Configuration Management
    5.2.3   Quality Management
    5.3   PROCESS ENVIRONMENT
    5.3.1   Organizational Structure
    5.3.2   External Interfaces
    5.3.3   Tools, Workbenches, & Environments
    5.3.4   Training
    5.3.5   Culture
6. AUDIT SUMMARY

Figure 6-1   SQPA Results Report outline

1. INTRODUCTION
2. BUSINESS ENVIRONMENT
3. RECOMMENDATIONS
    3.1   MODEL-RELATED RECOMMENDATIONS
    3.2   CONTROL-RELATED RECOMMENDATIONS
    3.3   ENVIRONMENTAL RECOMMENDATIONS
4. SUMMARY
5. CONCLUSION

Figure 6-2   SQPA Recommendations Report outline

evaluate the particular methodologies used by the audited organization and determine their effectiveness and efficiency based on the needs of the organization. Several project dependent factors are assessed to determine which quality issues are most critical and to determine needs. These factors include project size, newness, nature of the application, criticality to marketing, staff experience, customer expectations, quality reputation, product life cycle, and future expectations. It is left to the recipients of this report to collaborate in decisions establishing priorities and to chart a course of action.

Recommendations presented in this report are categorized, and presented, by the process perspective to which they apply. Specifically, they are:

- Model-related recommendations. Recommendations that relate directly to the process model are most easily implemented by those groups and individuals closest to the specific process involved. For this reason, these recommendations can often be the quickest to implement within a limited budget, and can provide immediate return on improvement efforts. The emphasis here is on doing things right.
- Control-related recommendations. As contrasted with model-related recommendations that can help individuals do things right, control-related recommendations can help individuals do the right things. Specifically, control allows the removal of roadblocks, consistency of process application, and the consolidation (and retention) of gains. Recommendations in this category tend to require a greater consistency of purpose, coordination at higher levels, and management commitment. Therefore, activities in response to these recommendations invest in our future rather than giving us immediate return on investment.
- Environmental recommendations. Definition and flow of control is crucial. So, however, is the consistency and flow of data (that is, communications paths, informal networks, information sources, et cetera). Recommendations that relate to the development process environment address information, the local culture, the existence or use of tools, and similar issues. Recommendations in this category can have a wide range of involvement with some only requiring local group consensus and others the support of upper management.

6.2.4 Executive Summary

Although there is a need to limit the ascent of unnecessary detail, a brief summary of audit activities, including an overview of recommendations, is typically published by the audit team (Figure 6-3).

6.2.5 Literary Suicide

Reports are intended to document and convey the minimum amount of information needed to understand and act on a situation. Results or recommendations (depending on the specific report being generated) must be sifted to identify the most important information. Reports that are too large, too detailed, or that

1. INTRODUCTION
2. BUSINESS ENVIRONMENT
3. SUMMARY OF FINDINGS
4. SUMMARY OF RECOMMENDATIONS
5. CONCLUSION

Figure 6-3 SQPA Executive Summary outline

fall short of addressing "real" issues are counterproductive. The quickest way to commit literary suicide (that is, losing your audience's respect) is to issue a document that contains any of the following phrases:

- "The audit team feels that . . . "
- "It appears that . . . "
- "We heard . . . "
- "Some people thought . . . "

The authoritative, though frank and unbiased, voice of your report must be maintained. Other report characteristics to avoid include:

- Judgmental: "The person was wrong to . . . "
- Omnipotent: "We have all **the** answers."
- Condemning: "Stupidity is what got you into this mess."
- Nagging: "We told you people before . . . "
- Possessive: "You people are only caretakers. We own the process."

When you write, do not forget that you are addressing a particular product or process, and not the person or team that developed or applied it. If there is evidence of such "people problems," look behind the symptoms to identify the ailment. Is the training process adequate to meet local needs? Is turnover (or the lack of it), attrition, or the communication network a problem? Do not violate trusts by mentioning names.

6.3 ROLE OF QUALITY MANAGEMENT

Quality Management is an active and rapidly evolving function within many companies, and it merits further attention before reviews and audits are discussed. A model for depicting software quality management activities is provided in Figure 6-4.

Activities are grouped using the framework {Perspective, Macro-Model Component, Activity Set} and examples are provided (Figure 6-5).

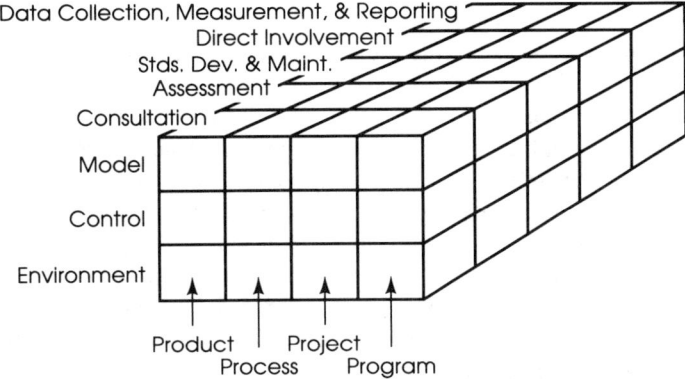

Figure 6-4 Characterizing the quality function

Perspective + Macro-Model Component + Activity Set	Sample Activity

Product +
  Model +
  Direct Involvement
	A document is a product. The quality department has the obligation to produce and maintain a Software Quality Assurance Plan as part of following the process model; they are directly involved.

Process +
  Model +
  Direct Involvement
	The quality department participates in the review of the Software Quality Assurance Plan.

Project +
  Control +
  Data Collection
  Measurement, &
  Reporting (DCM&R)
	The quality department for each project, to support control objectives, performs various DCM&R (that is, data collection, measurement, and reporting) activities.

Project +
  Control +
  Assessment
	The quality department for each project, to support control objectives, performs various audits.

Program +
  Control +
  Standards Development
  and Maintenance
	The quality department develops and maintains program level standards, such as minimum project documentation and reporting requirements.

Program +
  Environment +
  Direct Involvement
	The quality department has a key responsibility toward establishing and maintaining a quality culture. In this case, it is relative to ensuring that award and reward are attuned to process objectives.

Figure 6-5 Sample activities within the quality function taxonomy

Using the model improves the ability to characterize individual SQA organizations in terms of activities performed, thus providing an important extension to the knowledge base.

Why is this important? Because current wisdom provides no single solution to the quality equation. In fact, optimized return on your quality program investment, based on activities performed and services rendered, will change with your development program's maturity, its base process technology level, and the technology level inherent in the product mix. Whether as a tool in viewing what is done in other organizations, studying your own activity mix (or characterization), or as part of software quality program auditing (see Section 5.2.1), using the model can provide insight toward understanding what quality function activity alternatives exist and what does or does not work for you.

With respect to reviews and audits (R&A), some possible areas of activity are represented in Figure 6-6.

"Quality Management" has been used in our discussions to delay addressing the difference between quality assurance and quality control. The activity model presented in Figure 6-5 serves as a basis from which the discussion can be taken a step further: Quality assurance consists more of project and program related activities, whereas quality control focuses directly on distinct processes and products. Software Quality Assurance responsibilities would typically include documenting SQA policy set by upper management, auditing, and prescribing:

- General SQC policy and procedures
- Data collection, measurement, and reporting procedures
- Quality assurance measures for supplier-controlled development

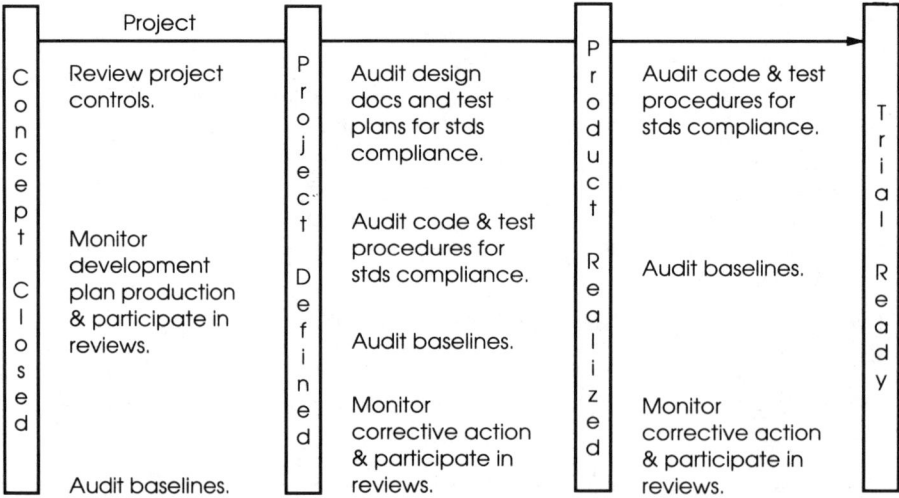

Figure 6-6 Typical quality mgt. involvement with reviews and audits

SQC relates to the continuous monitoring and reporting of conformance and performance objectives. The degree to which the product satisfies its requirements and to which standardized procedures are followed are the key conformance issues. Performance issues include productivity, problem management, and product reliability. Characteristic SQC responsibilities include:

- Monitoring the development process by conducting formal, standardized (internal) audits
- Providing periodic and special reports that detail conformance and performance
- Collaborating with project management to effect the expedient production of quality software

Recall the activity model of Figure 6-4. Not only can this taxonomy be used to describe quality management activities and assurance/control distinctions, but (with slight modification) it can also be applied to the realm of software related standards (Figure 6-7). Typically, standards come in three flavors:

1. Standard: "Thou shalt . . ."
2. Recommended practice: "You should . . ."
3. Convention (that is, common practice or guidance): "One way you can do it is . . ."

This reasoning has been presented to foster an appreciation for the audit report formats defined in Section 6.2 and associated samples in the appendixes.

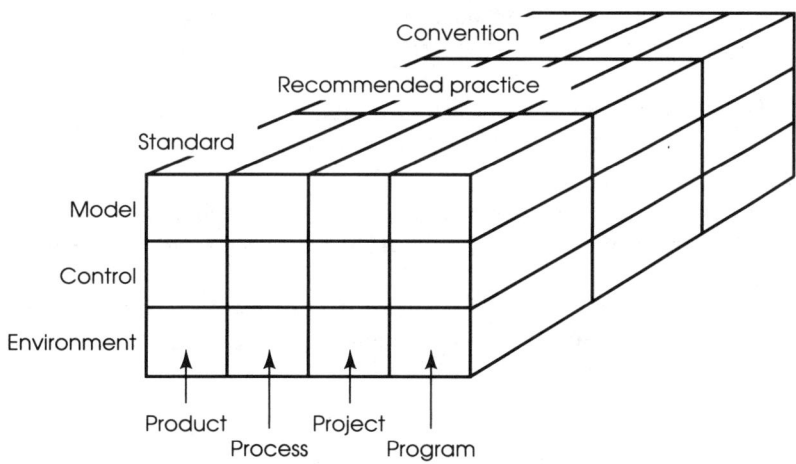

Figure 6-7 A standards taxonomy

CHAPTER 7
A Guess and A Vision

Everyone has a "vision" of where they and their company are headed. The vision this section refers to is *your* corporate vision. Most companies, in advancing their visionary goals, have encountered some common software development problems. To achieve "the vision," certain roadblocks must be overcome. Most roadblocks probably include model, control, and environmental elements that may in some way look like the following.

Model (the "Process" level):
- High production and maintenance costs (and low quality) of in-process documentation and customer deliverable documentation
- Inconsistent application of the review process
- The immaturity of software verification and validation planning
- Weaknesses in product planning and specification processes

Controls (the "Project" level):
- The uniform lack of sound configuration management (that is, configuration item identification, change control, status accounting, and configuration auditing)
- Strategic planning lacks software process goals and objectives
- The multitude of potentially overlapping and inconsistently applied project-level planning requirements

Environment (the "Program" level):
- The lack of corporate software process technology planning
- The lack of an integrated, though hierarchical (that is, Standard, Recommended Practice, Common Practice) network of standards on which to base program evolution and auditing activities

- Communication roadblocks from the geographic distribution of project responsibilities

This chapter provides guidance on managing your program to achieve your corporate "vision."

7.1 THE VISION AND THE JOURNEY

There is a need for a "new emphasis" on controlled process evolution. With new product technologies on the way, the need for new process technologies must be recognized. The ability to migrate to those new process technologies in an organized way is of great importance in achieving your vision. Failure there would directly affect margin. This point was illustrated in Chapter 2 when process improvement project reviews were introduced.

The journey ahead is one to search out and apply process technology breakthroughs to achieve the vision. Key elements of this effort include:

- Process improvement program
- Knowledge base maintenance
- Award and reward
- Decision support

7.2 PROGRAM OVERVIEW

Critical process improvement program steps (Figure 7-1) are:

1. Seek: Adopt and implement a continuous process benchmarking policy.
2. Design: Promote a process design philosophy with emphasis on the total solution system (process technology profile).
3. Transition: Migrate to the new or improved technology profile while providing for consistency of application and the demonstration of process compliance and performance.
4. Maintain: Consolidate gains and establish a process problem reporting and corrective action program.

Senior commitment and participation at the lowest levels of decision making is prerequisite. A typical improvement project within this framework would exhibit major milestones similar to those for any product realization project. Refer back to the discussion of process improvement project reviews in Chapter 3 and the project checklists found in the appendixes.

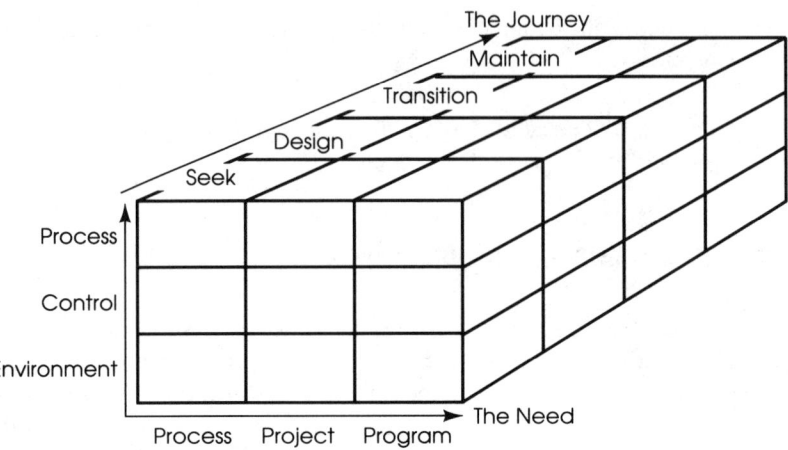

Figure 7-1 Achieving the vision

7.3 KNOWLEDGE BASE MAINTENANCE

Having established a mechanism for controlled process change, the knowledge base must be maintained. This means getting and keeping good people. Planned effort should go into the following activities:

- Track and analyze attrition losses.
- Provide on-the-job training (OJT) and back-fill.
- Renew emphasis on skill development.
- Improve recruiting.
- Establish protected rotation to key areas.
- Establish "corridor" entry levels.
- Schedule regular company conferences to communicate policy and objectives, and to stimulate technical exchange.

7.4 AWARD AND REWARD

A common theme in having your change mechanism work and in maintaining your knowledge base is award and reward. Knowing what should be done and then getting it done assumes that reward is consistent with process objectives.

Therefore, it is critical to establish a reward system consistent with software process objectives at the engineering, supervisory, and managerial levels.

A common bad example prevalent in industry is that people get rewarded for speedy one-time authorship and their ability to get on to something else. Emphasis needs to shift toward updating and redistributing commercial (or product) specifications.

A good example is set by development managers who truly understand the inspection process and how to use it for maximum benefit. Unlike those who expect, and reward people for producing, products that receive a disposition of *"1—publish as noted without further verification,"* these managers understand the economies of a bell-shaped distribution for inspection results. (Refer to the definition of the inspection process in Chapter 4.)

Staff hours expended for the inspection of a design document allow further examination of this topic. A typical inspection meeting might require the time of four people, each preparing for two hours and then attending a two-hour meeting. Total time spent in support on the inspection is 16 hours, or two days. The author has an important decision to make: When should the meeting be scheduled? If the goal is to receive only category-1 dispositions, there is a motivation to avoid the risk of receiving a different disposition for the product, and spending several days on fine-tuning seems wise. Unfortunately, there is still no guarantee that rework can be avoided. In fact, the risk of substantial rework increases with the amount of time that passes before the author receives the peer input afforded by the inspecton process. Figure 7-2 provides a graphic comparison between timely inspection and inspection delayed because of misdirected reward.

7.5 DECISION SUPPORT

Successful navigation does not happen by chance alone; decisions will have to be made. Well informed decision makers are crucial to your corporate vison. The following recommendations are made in the area of decision support:

- Standardize reporting schemes for product and process metrics.
- Establish a mechanism for reporting process compliance.
- Maintain and publish process characterizations for each program.

	Tune	Schedule & Study	Meet	Rework	Schedule & Study	Meet	TOTAL
Perfectionism	5	7	1/4	1	0	0	13+ Calendar days
	5	1	1	1	0	0	8 Staff days
Perfectionism gone wrong	5	7	1/4	5	7	1/4	24+ Calendar days
	5	1	1	5	1	1	14 Staff days
Timely inspection (worst case)	0	7	1/4	3	7	1/4	17+ Calendar days
	0	1	1	3	1	1	7 Staff days

Figure 7-2 Economies of timing

- Establish metrics policy and guidance that addresses all information opportunities (Figure 7-3).

Critical to modeling and the development of metrics is that they be developed (and committed to) with an understanding of:

- Fitness for use. The management decisions they can support.
- Cost/Benefit. The value added to the decision-making process.
- Problem Partitioning. The interactions and relationships between metrics (for example, what subset of popular metrics is necessary and sufficient to ...).
- Data Verification. How confidence is established that the "numbers" are the right numbers.
- Data Validation. How it is known that data elements are of the proper type and within defined ranges, or "meaningful."
- Process Preservation. The act of nondestructive measurement.
- Process Design. Designing the processes with measurement in mind. For consistency and comparison, data collection must only occur at process control points.

7.6 RECOMMENDATIONS

Although many of the problems stated in this chapter may not exist in your organization or may already be recognized and addressed, they nonetheless are all too prevalent in industry, resulting in the following conclusions:

Process			Product	
Resources expended	Environmental characteristics	Defect management	Static characteristics	Behavioral characteristics
		• Number		
• Human effort	• Methods	• Cause		
• Computer res.	• Tools	• Effect	• Size	• Failure rate
• Special trng.	• Personnel	• Fix integrity	• Complexity	• Throughput
• Other costs	• Application	• Fix on fix	• Timing	• Duration

Figure 7-3 Measurement opportunities

Improved Processes: The emphasis here is on *doing things right*. Process model related improvements are most easily implemented by those groups and individuals closest to the specific process involved. These improvements are the quickest to implement within a limited budget, and can provide immediate return on improvement efforts. Corporate should provide guidance and remove roadblocks.

Improved Controls: The emphasis here is on *doing the right things*. Control allows the removal of roadblocks, consistency of process application, and the consolidation (and retention) of gains. Control changes require a greater consistency of purpose, coordination at higher levels, and management commitment. This invests in our future rather than giving us immediate return on investment. Corporate should provide motivation and negotiate change.

Improved Environment: Emphasis here is on the motivation and ability to perform. This addresses the consistency and flow of information, the local culture, the existence or use of tools, and similar issues. There is a wide range of involvement with some objectives only requiring local group consensus, and others the support or involvement of corporate management. Corporate should initiate and orchestrate improvement.

APPENDIX 1
CHECKLISTS

The function of this appendix is to provide a workbook, not a cookbook. Checklists representative of what you might need are provided as a starting point that can be examined and edited to meet your needs. They may not be complete or appropriate for a particular organization or project.

In fact, you will note that vendor or subcontractor issues and controls have not been addressed. This intentional omission removes a layer of complexity and makes it easier to focus on your own immediate review and audit needs. Once your framework is established, it can be expanded to reflect those extra considerations.

Also germane here is the treatment of hardware issues. Included superficially in the treatment of project checklists, hardware issues identified here are included to preserve an awareness that systems are developed, deployed, and supported. The risks involved with single-sourcing may be a good example of what you may have to add. Your particular situation will guide you in editing checklists to provide coverage adequate for your needs.

Also missing are product checklists for any planning documents. Effective planning provides an appropriate treatment of control issues and can vary in detail, the number of distinct (yet interwoven) planning efforts documented, and specific project control requirements. Planning documents found in the literature are too numerous to address and doing so would result in so many planning document checklists that underlying control needs might be lost. Having the best documented poor plans should be avoided and fragmented or redundant representations that are difficult to implement or verify should be prevented.

Further guidance on the preparation and use of checklists includes:

- Be generous with the use of "i.e." and "e.g." lists. This promotes the understanding of specific questions and associated responses.

- Keep your list manageably small for its intended user. Some pruning will be required.
- Binary response lists should be used only where a quick answer is required on an obvious issue. You may want to rework some subset of your checklists to reflect a range of responses from "strongly agree" to "strongly disagree."
- Modify checklists as needed at the beginning of each audit. If left until interviews have begun, severe administrative problems may occur.

Another aspect of writing and using checklists is the language used. A mixture of phrasing approaches has been used here and consistent wording for a given application is recommended. Wording can also be revised to keep in step with the needs of your program. For example, a different response might be received if you were to substitute the word "known" in the statement below with "documented," "accurate," or "acceptable."

yes no
☐ ☐   Requirements are known.

PROGRAM CHECKLISTS

> ☑ **Process Definition**
>
> **Development life cycle model**
>
> yes no
> ☐ ☐ Overview is documented.
> ☐ ☐ Each stage has clear contribution.
> ☐ ☐ Each stage has well-defined entry criteria.
> ☐ ☐ Each stage has well-defined exit criteria.
> ☐ ☐ Each stage has well-defined deliverables.
> ☐ ☐ There is a requirement that each of the software requirements shall be defined, such that its achievement is capable of being objectively verified by a prescribed method (e.g., for inspection, demonstration, analysis, or test).
> ☐ ☐ There is a requirement that a document be provided describing the major components of the software design, including databases and internal interfaces.
> ☐ ☐ There is a requirement that an expansion of this description be included to describe each subcomponent of the major components.
> ☐ ☐ Deliverables are clearly identified as to whether they are configuration items.
> ☐ ☐ Problem Reporting and Corrective Action (PRCA) procedures are well documented and are consistent with whether the software element in question is or is not a configuration item.
> ☐ ☐ Problem Reporting and Corrective Action (PRCA) procedures are followed.
> ☐ ☐ Problem Reporting and Corrective Action (PRCA) are consistent across stages and organizations.
> ☐ ☐ How to interface with change control support systems is defined.
> ☐ ☐ All stage responsibilities are defined and understood.
> ☐ ☐ All major liaisons are known and controlled.
> ☐ ☐ A formal Software Development Plan (SDP) is required for each project.

✓ Process Definition (cont.)

Verification and Validation

yes	no	
☐	☐	V&V tasks and development tasks are well integrated.
☐	☐	The products of each development stage are verified as conforming to applicable standards and verified as consistent with the intent of the previous stage.
☐	☐	The end product is validated as complying with established software and system requirements.
☐	☐	There is a requirement that the document describe the methods (i.e., inspection, demonstration, analysis, or test) to be used to verify that the code, when executed, meets the previously documented requirements.
☐	☐	V&V tasks are iteratively applied to ensure the integrity of all baselines and their evolution.
☐	☐	More than one review process type is used.
☐	☐	Reviews and audits are well defined.
☐	☐	Reviews and audits are actually held and documented.

☐	☐	Test process deliverables have been defined to include:
		    Test Plans (mapping to various levels of product abstraction),
		    Test Design Specifications, Test Case Specifications,
		    Test Procedure Specifications, Test Item Transmittal Reports,
		    Test Logs, Test Incident Reports, Test Summary Reports,
		    Test input data and output data. Test Tools may also be included.

☐	☐	A formal Software Verification and Validation Plan (SVVP) is required for each project.
☐	☐	Task completion reports document progress against the SVVP, interim results, and problem status.
☐	☐	An anomaly report contains the description and location, impact, probable cause, severity, and recommendation.
☐	☐	A stage completion report summarizes tasks performed, task results, anomalies and their resolution, degree of deviation from the SVVP, and a statement of software quality.

☑ Process Controls

General Controls

yes no
- ☐ ☐ Standards, practices, and conventions are adhered to.
- ☐ ☐ Effectiveness is monitored.
- ☐ ☐ Efficiency is monitored.
- ☐ ☐ Motivation and reward are consistent with goals and objectives.
- ☐ ☐ You know your most frequent problems.

Software Quality Management

yes no
- ☐ ☐ Internal software quality assurance function.
- ☐ ☐ Independent of the development group.
- ☐ ☐ Authority documented and understood.
- ☐ ☐ Other organizations know how to interface with them.

Software Configuration Management (SCM)

yes no
- ☐ ☐ Formal configuration management plans.
- ☐ ☐ SCM includes: configuration item (CI) identification, change control, auditing, and status reporting.
- ☐ ☐ Entry into and exit from CI status is controlled.
- ☐ ☐ No unauthorized changes can be made.
- ☐ ☐ Completeness and correctness of a particular configuration ensured.

Well-defined Project Management Function

yes no
- ☐ ☐ Project management covers all development.
- ☐ ☐ Project leader at a sufficient level of authority.
- ☐ ☐ Milestones are established and funds are available to do the work.
- ☐ ☐ There is tracking and reporting of the work progress.
- ☐ ☐ Project management is proactive rather than reactive.

✓ Quality Management

Standards

yes no

☐ ☐ There is a requirement for identifying the standards, practices, and conventions to be applied.

☐ ☐ The differences between the levels of applicable standards (i.e., the difference between full standard, recommended practice, and common practice) are described.

☐ ☐ There is a requirement to state how compliance to these items is to be monitored and ensured.

Planning

yes no

☐ ☐ There is a requirement that an Executive Program Review be planned and held periodically to assess the execution of SQA and other project control plans.

☐ ☐ There is a requirement that these reviews be held by an organizational element independent of the unit being audited or by a qualified third party.

☐ ☐ The Divisional Quality Manual provides requirements for the preparation and content of SQA plans.

☐ ☐ SQA plans are required for the development and maintenance of all critical software (that is, where failure could impact on safety or cause large financial or social losses).

☐ ☐ There is a requirement that the plan be authenticated by the Chief Operating Officer of each unit of the organization having responsibilities defined in the plan.

☐ ☐ There is a requirement that the SQA plan have a section(s) specifying its purpose, scope, and retirement.

☐ ☐ There is a requirement that the names of the software product items covered by the SQA plan be listed (i.e., by marketed name, internal nomenclature, specific issue, and so on).

☐ ☐ There is a requirement that the intended use of the software item be listed.

☐ ☐ There is a requirement that the special software tools, techniques, and methodologies employed on this specific report that supports QA be identified, have their purposes stated, and have their use described.

☑ Quality Management (cont.)

Assessment

yes	no	
☐	☐	There is a requirement that the tasks associated with all software life cycle phases be described with specific emphasis on SQA activities and their sequence.
☐	☐	There is a requirement that the documentation governing the development, verification, use, and maintenance of the software be identified.
☐	☐	There is a requirement that a statement be made on how the documents are to be checked for adequacy and by whom.
☐	☐	There is a requirement that the review or audit be identified, by which the adequacy of each document shall be confirmed.
☐	☐	There is a requirement that a document be provided that clearly and precisely describes each of the essential requirements (e.g., functions, performances, design constraints, and attributes of the software and the interfaces).
☐	☐	There is a requirement that a document be provided describing the results of executing the software verification and validation plan.
☐	☐	There is a requirement that this document include the results of specified reviews, audits, and tests.
☐	☐	There is a requirement that an audit be held prior to software delivery to verify that all requirements specified in the previous documentation have been met.
☐	☐	There is a requirement that an audit to verify that the software and its documentation are internally consistent and ready for delivery.
☐	☐	There is a requirement that in-process audits of the design be held to verify consistence of the design, including: Code versus design documentation, interface specifications, design implementation versus functional requirements, functional requirements versus test descriptions.
☐	☐	There is a requirement that the supplier be required to prepare and implement an SQA plan in accordance with IEEE Standard 730 or its equivalent.
☐	☐	There is a requirement for stating provisions to ensure vendor-provided and subcontractor-developed software meets established technical requirements.

☑ Configuration Management

General Requirements

yes no
☐ ☐ There is a requirement for documenting methods used to identify the software product items, control and implement changes, and record and report change implementation status.
☐ ☐ There is a requirement for documenting practices and procedures required to report software problems, track software problems, and resolve software problems.
☐ ☐ There is a requirement for documenting the predelivery practices and procedures required to report software problems, track software problems, and resolve software problems.
☐ ☐ There is a requirement for documenting the postdelivery practices and procedures required to report software problems, track software problems, and resolve software problems.
☐ ☐ There is a requirement for specifying organizational responsibilities in problem reporting and corrective action.
☐ ☐ There is a requirement for describing methods and facilities used to maintain and store controlled versions of identified software.
☐ ☐ There is a requirement for describing methods and facilities used to protect computer program physical media from unauthorized access or inadvertent damage or degradation.

Configuration Item (CI) Identification

yes no
☐ ☐ Standards and procedures manuals.
☐ ☐ Software requirements specifications.
☐ ☐ Software design descriptions, by level of product abstraction.
☐ ☐ Test documentation, by level of product abstraction.
☐ ☐ Software verification plans.
☐ ☐ Software verification reports.
☐ ☐ Configuration management plan.
☐ ☐ Software quality assurance plan.
☐ ☐ Documentation index.
☐ ☐ User guides and manuals.
☐ ☐ Training procedures (internal and user).

✓ Configuration Management (cont.)

CI Change Control

yes no

☐ ☐ Procedures ensure that the (CI declared) documentation is kept current, usable, complete, and consistent.
☐ ☐ Procedures ensure that (CI declared) code is current, usable, complete, and consistent.
☐ ☐ Procedures ensure that (CI declared) test scripts are kept current, usable, complete, and consistent.

CI Change Documentation

☐ ☐ Overview of the change control system
☐ ☐ Description of all user/software interfaces
☐ ☐ Data entry procedures (requirements and format)
☐ ☐ Mechanics for reporting and correcting change control system problems
☐ ☐ Mechanism for reporting and fixing CI problems

CI Auditing

☐ ☐ Documentation periodically reviewed or audited.
☐ ☐ All of the identified documentation exists.
☐ ☐ All of the identified documentation is used.
☐ ☐ All of the identified documentation is current.
☐ ☐ You have what you think you have.

Status Accounting

☐ ☐ Reports reflect how documentation is evolving.
☐ ☐ CI status is periodically reviewed or audited.
☐ ☐ You are getting closer to what you want.

CM System User Documentation

☐ ☐ Overview of the software system.
☐ ☐ Description of all user/software interfaces.
☐ ☐ Data entry procedures (requirements and format).
☐ ☐ Mechanics for reporting and fixing user problems.

✓ Project Management

General Requirements

yes no

☐ ☐ There is a requirement that, for each project, a coherent set of valid planning documents be generated and implemented.

☐ ☐ These plans are placed under change control and are kept both current and consistent with each other and the realities of the project.

☐ ☐ There is a requirement that a complete list of documents referenced elsewhere in the text of any plan be provided, and that those documents be kept current and available.

☐ ☐ Guidelines exist for the selection, generation, review, and implementation of these plans.

☐ ☐ These plans are consistent with the project baseline.

☐ ☐ Project planning documentation includes information spanning project, system development, product assurance (CM, QA), verification and validation, and delivery/support/service planning activities.

☐ ☐ Progress information is adequate for measurement, control, and continuous process improvement.

☐ ☐ Cost information is adequate for measurement, control, and continuous process improvement.

☐ ☐ There is a requirement for rigorous contract administration and control.

Project Organization

yes no

☐ ☐ There is a requirement that the total organizational structure influencing software quality be presented:
  - With a pictorial overview
  - With every major element and its delegated responsibilities described
  - With organizational dependence or independence of SQA clearly depicted

☐ ☐ There is a well-defined relationship between the project manager and the functional managers.

☑ Project Management (cont.)

Project Manager

yes no
☐ ☐ A project manager of adequate authority has been named.
☐ ☐ The project manager approves the functional department's general plan to accomplish project work.
☐ ☐ The project manager prepares and maintains the project's master plan. This includes major tasks, schedules, and budgets for all participating organizational elements.

Managing the Work

yes no
☐ ☐ Adequate schedule provisions have been made for special training, turnover, vacation, formal schooling, health care, and process improvement project involvement.
☐ ☐ Adequate schedule provisions have been made for appraisal and rework activities.
☐ ☐ Scheduled milestones are required for delivery of work products, methodology driven events, and project termination.
☐ ☐ Scheduled milestones are required for project finance events such as project funding, budget reviews, and revenue events (i.e., order, sale, delivery, payment, penalty, and warranty).
☐ ☐ There is a requirement that milestone descriptions include a due date or algorithm that determines the due date, current cost budget, completion criteria, and evaluation and acceptance criteria.

✓ Process Environment

Tools, Workbenches, and Environments

yes no
- ☐ ☐ Specific environments, workbenches, and tools are well defined.
- ☐ ☐ Their use is monitored and supported.
- ☐ ☐ Their development is controlled. Change control is in place.
- ☐ ☐ Shortcomings of labs are known and compensated for.
- ☐ ☐ Lab use controlled and documented.
- ☐ ☐ Tools, workbenches, and environments support and are not in conflict with product and process standards.
- ☐ ☐ Wherever possible, standards and recommended practices have been embodied in the tools, workbenches, and environments. Thus, process control has been effectively delegated to the process environment.

People

yes no
- ☐ ☐ Training is adequate and managed adequately.
- ☐ ☐ Expertise is routinely passed on to the next person.
- ☐ ☐ Recognition, reward, and advancement is consistent with process objectives.

☑ Information Management

Measurement and Evaluation

yes no

☐ ☐ Measurements and evaluations are fit for use. They directly support important decisions.

☐ ☐ The benefit of measurement and evaluation outweighs cost. They add value to the decision-making process.

☐ ☐ Information needs are documented and mapped (partitioned) to standard metric definitions as required. Metrics used are a subset of those defined. The interactions and relationships between metrics (e.g., what subset of well defined metrics is necessary and sufficient to ...) is documented and understood.

☐ ☐ Data are verified. Confidence is established and maintained that the "numbers" are the right numbers (they have the right meaning).

☐ ☐ Data are validated. It is known that data elements are of the proper type and within defined ranges, or "meaningful."

☐ ☐ Measurement is nondestructive. The process is preserved.

☐ ☐ The processes are designed with measurement and evaluation in mind. For consistency and comparison, data collection occurs only at process control points.

Nomenclature and Labeling

yes no

☐ ☐ A mandatory labeling standard exists and provides for version and revision identification for each product and release.

☐ ☐ The hierarchy in the baseline held by each entity is reflected by its nomenclature.

☐ ☐ All modifiable entities are afforded naming conventions that will reflect their status.

☐ ☐ Unit and file naming conventions are maintained.

☑ Information Management (cont.)

Project Libraries

yes	no	
☐	☐	There is a requirement to identify the project documentation to be retained.
☐	☐	There is a requirement to identify the methods and facilities to be used to assemble, safeguard, and maintain the project documentation.
☐	☐	There is a requirement to identify the retention period and access levels of said project documentation.
☐	☐	Records are secure from (or can be reconstructed after) disaster, deliberate damage, and theft.
☐	☐	Provisions have been made for backup and reconstruction.
☐	☐	Library storage and administration procedures enforce and support change control and baseline auditing.
☐	☐	Library storage and administration procedures enforce and support publication distribution and access rules.
☐	☐	There is a "programmer's" library for managing newly created or modified software entities. It is controlled by generation activities.
☐	☐	There is a "control" library for managing the current baseline and its changes. Items are promoted by a change control board into this library from the programmer's library.
☐	☐	There is "release" library for archiving various baselines released for general use.

✓ Program Evolution

Product Technology

yes	no	
☐	☐	The quality program provides assurance that the chosen technology is appropriate, feasible, and properly implemented.
☐	☐	The advancement of product technology as a step function is understood.
☐	☐	The changing economics of new product introduction along the current step function plateau is understood.

Process Technology

yes	no	
☐	☐	The quality program ensures that the chosen technology is appropriate, feasible, consistently applied, and properly supported.
☐	☐	The quality program ensures that the advancement of process technology is understood as either evolutionary or revolutionary.
☐	☐	Process technology's relationship to the cost of quality curves is understood.
☐	☐	Process improvement projects are supported and well managed.

Improvement Program

yes	no	
☐	☐	Problem Reporting and Corrective Action (PRCA) for processes is as formal as PRCA for the products they provide.
☐	☐	This Process PRCA is part of a funded, formal, continuous improvement program.
☐	☐	The continuous improvement program elements include management commitment and documented procedures.
☐	☐	The Continuous Improvement Program is supported by corporate policy, a dedicated facilitator, and the company's reward structure.

PROJECT CHECKLISTS FOR PRODUCT REALIZATION

☑ **Executive Project Evaluation**

Project "X" Snapshot

- General Market Availability
- Trial Readiness
- Product Realization
- Project Definition
- Concept Closure

Condition: *Red*

Issues:
- Review held and failed—adjustment in progress.
- Market analysis incomplete—position to market unclear.
- Funding and resource utilization inadequately planned.

The Marketplace

yes no
☐ ☐ Benefit to the customer is known.
☐ ☐ Customer motivation to purchase is understood.
☐ ☐ The Products place in the current product line is documented and understood, as is the product's impact on other company product lines.
☐ ☐ Requested R&D will provide all features necessary to secure stated sales.
☐ ☐ We know exactly what we are developing/enhancing, and why.
☐ ☐ Adequate customer communication/feedback mechanisms exist.

☑ Executive Project Evaluation (cont.)

The Marketing Effort

yes no
- ☐ ☐ Market research has been adequate and accurate.
- ☐ ☐ Any differences in customer/end-user markets is understood.
- ☐ ☐ Any change in the projected market size since the last review has been reported.
- ☐ ☐ Our advantages/disadvantages relative to our competitors' are understood.
- ☐ ☐ The distribution strategy is compatible with current channels and is supported by plans to develop/improve them.
- ☐ ☐ Pricing strategy is reasonable, manageable, and achievable in light of competition and market conditions.
- ☐ ☐ We know how our customers are reacting.
- ☐ ☐ We know how our competitors are reacting.

The Product

- ☐ ☐ Product changes, if any, from last review period have been explained and justified. The incremental revenue has been estimated/reported.
- ☐ ☐ The current development/enhancement represents a significant technical advance. Process and product technology barriers have been identified and are being managed.
- ☐ ☐ The financial impact of delaying the roll-out of the R&D product/features is understood and contingencies are planned for appropriately.
- ☐ ☐ The schedule for new product introduction compares favorably against knowledge of the competition.
- ☐ ☐ Major project milestones exist and progress has been reported. Success against the milestones is acceptable. Any schedule changes since last review have been reported.

Ability to Deliver

- ☐ ☐ Products and services will be delivered on time.
- ☐ ☐ The final cost will be within budget.
- ☐ ☐ Delivered product quality is predicted and all performance requirements will be met.
- ☐ ☐ The customer is pleased with progress.

✓ Concept Closure: Preparation Areas

Red	Yellow	Green	Description	Comments
☐	☐	☐	**The Product** • Envisioned product is defined.	
☐	☐	☐	**The Process** • Product is technically feasible.	
☐	☐	☐	**The Project** • Financial targets are established. • Project controls are outlined.	
☐	☐	☐	**The (Business) Environment** • Product strategy is sound.	

✓ Concept Closure: The Product

Envisioned product is defined.

yes no
☐ ☐   General product requirements specification has been written and reviewed.
☐ ☐   Feature descriptions have been written and reviewed.
☐ ☐   A system architecture has been outlined.

✓ Concept Closure: The Process

The product is technically feasible.

yes no
☐ ☐   Feasibility study report supports the development effort.
☐ ☐   Product technology has been characterized.
☐ ☐   Process technology has been characterized.

☑ **Concept Closure: The Project**

Financial targets are established.

yes no
☐   ☐   Funding and resource utilization is adequately planned.

Project controls are outlined.

yes no
☐   ☐   Adequately detailed Project Management Plan Draft has been written and reviewed.
☐   ☐   Adequately detailed Quality Management Plan Draft has been written and reviewed.
☐   ☐   Adequately detailed Configuration Management Plan Draft has been written and reviewed.

☑ **Concept Closure: (Business) Environment**

The product strategy is sound.

yes no
☐   ☐   Position to market has been stated.
☐   ☐   Target markets have been identified.
☐   ☐   Potential customers have been identified.
☐   ☐   Value to customer has been established.
☐   ☐   Sales potential (products and services) has been projected.

✓ Project Definition: Preparation Areas

Red	Yellow	Green	Description	Comments
☐	☐	☐	**The Product** • The product definition is adequate.	
☐	☐	☐	**The Process** • The development process is in place.	
☐	☐	☐	**The Project** • Financial targets are refined. • Project controls are detailed. • The project environment is planned.	
☐	☐	☐	**The (Business) Environment** • Market strategy is sound. • Market roll-out is planned. • Competitive analysis has been completed.	

✓ Project Definition: The Product

Product definition is adequate.

yes	no	
☐	☐	General product requirements specification is fit for use.
☐	☐	System design specification is fit for use.
☐	☐	Software requirements specification is fit for use.
☐	☐	The product technology is adequately understood.
☐	☐	The product's position in the overall product mix is understood.
☐	☐	Hardware/software tradeoffs have been examined.
☐	☐	Software size and complexity have been estimated.
☐	☐	Circuit pack count and complexity have been estimated.

☑ **Project Definition: The Process**

The development process is in place.

yes no
☐ ☐ The Software Development Plan is fit for use.
☐ ☐ The User Documentation Plan is fit for use.
☐ ☐ The User Support Plan is fit for use.
☐ ☐ The Load Build and Configuration Control Plan is fit for use.
☐ ☐ The Software Verification and Validation Plan is fit for use.
☐ ☐ The System Test Plan is fit for use.
☐ ☐ The process technology is adequately understood.
☐ ☐ On further review, product feasibility is certain.
☐ ☐ Design priorities are documented.
☐ ☐ Maintenance and service requirements have been established.
☐ ☐ The manufacturing/media duplication plan is fit for use.

☑ **Project Definition: The Project**

Financial targets are refined.

yes no
☐ ☐ Subsystem cost targets have been documented and are consistent with other plans.
☐ ☐ R&D capital is available.
☐ ☐ Team resources are available and identified.
☐ ☐ Costs and yields have been projected.

Project controls are detailed.

yes no
☐ ☐ The Project Management Plan has been written and reviewed.
☐ ☐ The Quality Management Plan has been written and reviewed.
☐ ☐ The Configuration Management Plan has been written and reviewed.
☐ ☐ Training and customer support plans have been outlined.
☐ ☐ Installation plan has been outlined.

The project environment is planned.

yes no
☐ ☐ Necessary training has been identified.
☐ ☐ Adequate needs analysis and planning has taken place to ensure that appropriate tools, workbenches, and environments (TW&E) will be made available to those needing them.
☐ ☐ This planning has influenced the budgeting process.
☐ ☐ Adequate controls have been placed on tool definition, procurement, development, and support.
☐ ☐ TW&E planning has taken into consideration any need for performance modeling, simulation, prototyping assistance, design representation, and text processing with imbedded graphics.
☐ ☐ TW&E planning has taken into consideration any need for automated specification, code generation, source code reformatting, test case generation, and dynamic assertion.
☐ ☐ TW&E planning has taken into consideration any need for complexity analysis and code coverage analysis.
☐ ☐ TW&E planning has taken into consideration any need for supporting the control functions with effort and cost related tools to estimate, track, analyze, and report on the development effort.

☑ **Project Definition: (Business) Environment**

The market strategy is sound.

yes no
☐ ☐ Features have been prioritized by anticipated market value.
☐ ☐ Consensus on feature content, functionality, and performance has been reached with any established or trial use customers.

The market roll-out is planned.

yes no
☐ ☐ Potential customers have been identified.
☐ ☐ Customer satisfaction indices have been defined and prioritized, and the data collection, measurement, and reporting mechanism has been identified.
☐ ☐ Marketing commitments have been made.
☐ ☐ Marketing communications have been planned.

Competitive analysis has been completed.

yes no
☐ ☐ Necessary plan revisions have been initiated and approved.
☐ ☐ Competitive analysis has been revisited with regard to release timing.

☑ Product Realization: Preparation Areas

Red	Yellow	Green	Description	Comments
☐	☐	☐	**The Product** • The delivered product meets its specification.	
☐	☐	☐	**The Process** • Prescribed procedures were followed.	
☐	☐	☐	**The Project** • Financial targets are on track. • Project controls were correctly implemented.	
☐	☐	☐	**The (Business) Environment** • The marketing activity progresses.	

☑ Product Realization: The Product

The delivered product meets its specification.

yes	no	
☐	☐	Test Verification Reports have been distributed.
☐	☐	Review Reports have been studied.
☐	☐	The Delivered Product is complete.

☑ Product Realization: The Process

Prescribed procedures were followed.

yes no
- ☐ ☐ In-process audit reports verify conformance to process.
- ☐ ☐ Where exceptions have been noted, risk has been appraised.
- ☐ ☐ Prototypes have been evaluated with documented results.
- ☐ ☐ Prototype manufacturability has been assessed and results have been documented.

☑ Product Realization: The Project

Financial targets are on track.

yes no
- ☐ ☐ Subsystem cost targets have been met.

Project controls were correctly implemented.

yes no
- ☐ ☐ Training and customer support plans have been written and reviewed.
- ☐ ☐ Installation plan has been written and reviewed.
- ☐ ☐ The testing laboratory/testbed is adequately managed and has the appropriate tools and system configuration(s) available.

☑ Product Realization: (Business) Environment

The marketing activity progresses.

yes no
- ☐ ☐ The marketing strategy is sound.
- ☐ ☐ The market roll-out is planned.
- ☐ ☐ Competitive analysis has been completed.

✓	**Trial Readiness: Preparation Areas**	

Red	Yellow	Green	Description	Comments
☐	☐	☐	**The Product** • The specification framework is complete and current. • Postverification problem report status is acceptable. • Deliverables have been polished.	
☐	☐	☐	**The Process** • Prescribed procedures were followed. • Product verification has been completed. • Manufacturing channel preparation is adequate. • Delivery/service channel preparation is adequate.	
☐	☐	☐	**The Project** • Financial targets are on track. • Project controls were correctly implemented. • Trial plan has been reviewed and approved.	
☐	☐	☐	**The (Business) Environment** • The market strategy is sound. • Sales channel preparation is adequate.	

☑ Trial Readiness: The Product

The specification framework is complete and current.

yes no
☐ ☐ Baselines have been updated.
☐ ☐ Requirements, design, and test documentation is current and complete.
☐ ☐ The system is stable.

Post-verification problem report status is acceptable.

yes no
☐ ☐ Test Verification Reports have been distributed.
☐ ☐ Review Reports have been studied.
☐ ☐ Product churn has stabilized after incorporating changes.

Deliverables have been polished.

yes no
☐ ☐ Customer training and documentation has been written, reviewed, and approved.
☐ ☐ Feature functionality is complete and correctly implemented.
☐ ☐ No critical problem reports remain open.
☐ ☐ Adequate work-arounds exist for any significant problems that remain.

☑ **Trial Readiness: The Process**

Prescribed procedures were followed.

yes no
- ☐ ☐ In-process audit reports verify conformance to process.
- ☐ ☐ Where exceptions have been noted, risk has been appraised.

Product verification has been completed.

yes no
- ☐ ☐ Test verification report has been issued and reviewed.
- ☐ ☐ Software verification and validation plan execution results have been reviewed.
- ☐ ☐ The product is baselined and controlled.

Manufacturing channel preparation is adequate.

yes no
- ☐ ☐ The product is manufacturable.
- ☐ ☐ Any new processes in support or manufacturing have been documented, reviewed, approved, and implemented.
- ☐ ☐ Component status has been updated and is satisfactory.
- ☐ ☐ The field return rate has been projected.
- ☐ ☐ The inventory requirements are known.
- ☐ ☐ Yields have been predicted.

Delivery/service channel preparation is adequate.

yes no
- ☐ ☐ The product has been proven "installable."
- ☐ ☐ Shipment dates have tentatively been set and shown attainable.

✓ Trial Readiness: The Project

Financial targets are on track.

yes no
- ☐ ☐ Development cost targets have been met.
- ☐ ☐ Cost targets have been established for manufacturing, service, and maintenance.

Project controls were correctly implemented.

yes no
- ☐ ☐ Software manufacturing plan is finalized.
- ☐ ☐ Trial Plan has been reviewed and approved.
- ☐ ☐ Trial Success Criteria have been set.
- ☐ ☐ A reasonable evaluation mechanism is in place to judge results against success criteria.

The support environment is planned.

yes no
- ☐ ☐ Necessary training has been identified.
- ☐ ☐ Adequate needs analysis and planning has taken place to ensure that appropriate tools, workbenches, and environments (TW&E) will be made available to those needing them.
- ☐ ☐ This planning has influenced the budgeting process.
- ☐ ☐ Adequate controls have been placed on tool definition, procurement, development, and support.
- ☐ ☐ TW&E planning has taken into consideration any need for field performance analysis and tracking.
- ☐ ☐ TW&E planning has taken into consideration any need for diagnostics.
- ☐ ☐ TW&E planning has taken into consideration any need for system simulation.
- ☐ ☐ TW&E planning has taken into consideration any need for supporting the control functions with effort and cost-related tools to estimate, track, analyze, and report on the support effort.

✓ Trial Readiness: (Business) Environment

The market strategy is sound.

yes no
☐ ☐   Market penetration strategy is finalized.
☐ ☐   Marketing communications have been designed.
☐ ☐   Product announcement has been made.

Sales channel preparation is adequate.

yes no
☐ ☐   Sales forecasts have been updated.
☐ ☐   Lead customers have been identified and contacted.

☑ General Market Availability: Preparation Areas

Red 🔴	Yellow 🟡	Green 🟢	Description	Comments
☐	☐	☐	**The Product** • Specification framework is complete and current. • Posttrial problem report status is acceptable.	
☐	☐	☐	**The Process** • Prescribed procedures were followed. • Product trial has been completed. • The product is baselined and controlled. • Manufacturing channel preparation is adequate. • Delivery channel preparation is adequate.	
☐	☐	☐	**The Project** • Financial targets are on track. • Project controls were correctly implemented.	
☐	☐	☐	**The (Business) Environment** • The market strategy is sound. • Sales channel preparation is adequate.	

☑ General Market Availability: The Product

The specification framework is complete and current.

yes no
- ☐ ☐ All operation, maintenance, and support manuals are complete and consistent with the specification framework.
- ☐ ☐ The specification framework has been kept current and complete.
- ☐ ☐ The product meets regulatory and safety requirements.
- ☐ ☐ Design change histories are being documented.

Post Trial Problem Report status is acceptable.

- ☐ ☐ Trial Reports have been distributed.
- ☐ ☐ Review Reports have been studied.
- ☐ ☐ Environmental tests have been passed.
- ☐ ☐ Field return rates are acceptable.

☑ General Market Availability: The Process

Prescribed procedures were followed.

yes no
- ☐ ☐ In-process audit reports verify conformance to process.
- ☐ ☐ Where exceptions have been noted, risk has been appraised.

Product trial has been completed.
- ☐ ☐ The product (in all required configurations) has been adequately exercised in its operational environment.
- ☐ ☐ There are no unexpected operating system incompatibilities.
- ☐ ☐ Baselines are accurate, complete, and verified.
- ☐ ☐ Specific requirements have been mapped against trial site use and the sites, in combination, exercise all available features.

The product is baselined and controlled.
- ☐ ☐ During installation there have been no missing programs, files, or tools.
- ☐ ☐ No incorrect revisions have been supplied to the field.
- ☐ ☐ Both customer- and craft-deliverable documentation are complete with guidance and support evident.
- ☐ ☐ Work-arounds have been replaced by the appropriate fixes.

Manufacturing channel preparation is adequate.
- ☐ ☐ First-piece evaluations were successful.
- ☐ ☐ Out-of-box trial was successful.
- ☐ ☐ Yield projections have been updated.
- ☐ ☐ Manufacturability has been reaffirmed.

Delivery/service channel preparation is adequate.
- ☐ ☐ Installation instructions have proven adequate.
- ☐ ☐ All target machine configurations have been specified.
- ☐ ☐ Confirmation has been provided that installation has been proper and consistent.
- ☐ ☐ Correctness and completeness of installation package has been confirmed. This includes markings, warnings, labels, warranty information, and so on.
- ☐ ☐ Installed software has been confirmed as being the software that has undergone V&V.
- ☐ ☐ Service personnel are qualified.

☑ **General Market Availability: The Project**

Financial targets are on track.

yes no
☐ ☐ Development cost targets have been met.
☐ ☐ Maintenance costs, service volume, field return rate, and so on have all been projected.

Project controls were correctly implemented.

yes no
☐ ☐ Field trial was completed and documented.
☐ ☐ Field trial was successful against predetermined criteria.
☐ ☐ Controls are in place for standard configurations and custom configurations.
☐ ☐ Mechanism is in place to monitor customer satisfaction.
☐ ☐ Product costs are stabilizing.

☑ **General Market Availability: (Business) Environment**

The market strategy is sound.

yes no
☐ ☐ The market expansion strategy is reasonable.
☐ ☐ The market penetration rate is consistent with overall strategy.
☐ ☐ Marketing communications are proceeding according to plan.

Sales channel preparation is adequate.

yes no
☐ ☐ Ordering and pricing instructions have proven adequate.
☐ ☐ Sales forecast has been updated.
☐ ☐ Orders are being made.

✓ Product Maturity: Preparation Areas

Red	Yellow	Green	Description	Comments
☐	☐	☐	**The Product** • Specification framework is complete and current. • Product quality is stable and acceptable.	
☐	☐	☐	**The Process** • Prescribed procedures are routinely followed. • The product baseline remains under control. • Manufacturing channel response is adequate. • Delivery/support channel response is adequate.	
☐	☐	☐	**The Project** • Financial targets are on track. • Maintenance controls are currently implemented. • Operational support is adequate.	
☐	☐	☐	**The (Business) Environment** • The market strategy is sound. • Sales channel response is adequate.	

☑ **Product Maturity: The Product**

Specification framework is complete and current.

yes no
- ☐ ☐ Baselines are current, complete, and accurate.
- ☐ ☐ Deliverables are current and consistent.

Product quality is stable and acceptable.

yes no
- ☐ ☐ Capabilities have been modified, extended, or added as approved.
- ☐ ☐ Review Reports have been studied.
- ☐ ☐ Field performance is stable and acceptable.

☑ **Product Maturity: The Process**

Prescribed procedures are routinely followed.

yes no
- ☐ ☐ Corrective, perfective, and adaptive maintenance is performed with V&V and appropriate controls.
- ☐ ☐ All channels operate smoothly and follow standard procedures.

The product baseline remains under control.

yes no
- ☐ ☐ Audits confirm conformance to specification and adherence to standards.

Manufacturing channel response is adequate.

yes no
- ☐ ☐ Shipments are regularly scheduled and are made on time.
- ☐ ☐ Field return rates are acceptable.
- ☐ ☐ Yields are acceptable.
- ☐ ☐ Production costs are stable and acceptable.
- ☐ ☐ Cost reduction activities are underway and are proving successful.

Delivery/support channel response is adequate.

yes no
- ☐ ☐ Response to customer complaints and problems is adequate.

☑ Product Maturity: The Project

Financial targets are on track.

yes no
- ☐ ☐ Revenue targets are being met.
- ☐ ☐ Service costs are controlled.
- ☐ ☐ Production costs are controlled.

Maintenance controls are correctly implemented.

yes no
- ☐ ☐ Developers have received positive feedback on current process technologies and their specific application on this project.
- ☐ ☐ Problem escalation and response works smoothly.

Operational support is adequate.

yes no
- ☐ ☐ Customer training and support is adequate.
- ☐ ☐ Marketing communications are adequate.

☑ Product Maturity: (Business) Environment

The market strategy is sound.

yes no
- ☐ ☐ Profitability is adequate.
- ☐ ☐ Budget needs have been updated.
- ☐ ☐ Market penetration has occurred and market share is stabilizing.

Sales channel response is adequate.

yes no
- ☐ ☐ Sales forecasts have been updated.
- ☐ ☐ Sales volume is leveling off.
- ☐ ☐ Ordering and pricing guides remain accurate and adequate.

Product Retirement: Preparation Areas

Red / Yellow / Green	Description	Comments
☐ ☐ ☐	**The Product** • The specification framework is deteriorating. • Maintenance backlog is unacceptable.	
☐ ☐ ☐	**The Process** • Prescribed procedures are breaking down. • Product verification is increasingly difficult. • Manufacturing channel demand or response has slowed. • Delivery/service channel resources are strained.	
☐ ☐ ☐	**The Project** • Maintenance controls are faltering.	
☐ ☐ ☐	**The (Business) Environment** • The market strategy is being reexamined.	

☑ Product Retirement: The Product

The specification framework is deteriorating.

yes no
☐ ☐   The product has not been adapted to changes in external requirements.

Maintenance backlog is unacceptable.

yes no
☐ ☐   It is not feasible to correct defects that hinder continued service.
☐ ☐   Anomalies of increasing severity are being reported.

☑ Product Retirement: The Process

Prescribed procedures are breaking down.

yes no
☐ ☐   Manuals are losing their accuracy.
☐ ☐   Marketing, manufacturing, and service channels find it increasingly difficult to act in concert.

Product verification is increasingly difficult.

yes no
☐ ☐   Regression testing results provide less confidence.
☐ ☐   Fix integrity has declined.
☐ ☐   Fix-on-Fix has increased.
☐ ☐   The product baseline is becoming vague.

Manufacturing channel demand or response has slowed.

yes no
☐ ☐   Production volumes and yields are no longer stable.

Delivery/service channel resources are strained.

yes no
☐ ☐   Customer configurations are increasingly numerous and hard to track.
☐ ☐   Product upgrades are less desirable to the customer.
☐ ☐   Service costs and revenues are unbalanced.

☑ Product Retirement: The Project

Maintenance controls are faltering.

yes no
☐ ☐ The escalation mechanism is being bypassed.
☐ ☐ The maintenance effort is backlogged and not responsive.
☐ ☐ Priorities are increasingly difficult to establish.

☑ Product Retirement: (Business) Environment

The market strategy is being reexamined.

yes no
☐ ☐ Requests for modified, extended, or additional capabilities have been evaluated as not being economical/feasible.
☐ ☐ The product does not respond to its changing operational environment.
☐ ☐ Sales channel activity has diminished.
☐ ☐ Profitability is maintained below targeted internal rate of return (IRR).

PROJECT CHECKLISTS FOR PROCESS IMPROVEMENT

☑ Executive Project Evaluation

Sample Project Snapshot

- Remedy Transitioned
- Remedy Proven
- Remedy Trial Ready
- Cause Definition
- Project Sponsorship

Condition: Red

Issues:
- Review held and failed—adjustment in progress.
- Market analysis incomplete—position to market unclear.
- Funding and resource utilization inadequately planned.

General Considerations

yes no
☐   ☐   Open communication.
☐   ☐   Standard procedures followed.

The Project Authorization

yes no
☐   ☐   Established.
☐   ☐   Followed.

Progress

yes no
☐   ☐   Well Planned.
☐   ☐   Proceeding according to plan.

The Team

yes no
☐   ☐   Organized, communicative, and effective.

☑ PIP Project Sponsorship: Preparation Areas

Red	Yellow	Green	Description	Comments
☐	☐	☐	**The Team** • A team has been formed.	
☐	☐	☐	**The Improvement** • An improvement project has been chosen. • The improvement area products have adequately been studied. • The improvement area processes have adequately been studied.	
☐	☐	☐	**The Work** • A charter has been established. • The charter is reasonable.	

☑ PIP Project Sponsorship: The Team

A team has been formed.

yes	no	
☐	☐	A team has been formed and members listed.
☐	☐	Organizations represented by team members have been identified.
☐	☐	A team leader has been identified.
☐	☐	Any current plans for changing leadership after cause definition have been documented.
☐	☐	Member selection criteria have been documented.
☐	☐	Alternatives have been examined for assigning the responsibility for diagnosis.

☑ PIP Project Sponsorship: The Improvement

An improvement project has been chosen.

yes no
☐ ☐ The problem area targeted for improvement is well defined.
☐ ☐ The reason for addressing this area is supported.
☐ ☐ Reasonable criteria were used for area selection.

The improvement area products have been adequately studied.

yes no
☐ ☐ Work area outputs have been defined and their customers identified.
☐ ☐ Current requirements and feedback paths have been identified.
☐ ☐ Customer expectations have been documented.
☐ ☐ The approach and tools used to determine customer expectations were reasonable and adequate.
☐ ☐ The expectation gap has been described.

The improvement area processes have been adequately studied.

yes no
☐ ☐ The current process has been baselined and its flow depicted.
☐ ☐ Rework, work-arounds, and recurring problems have been identified.
☐ ☐ Current controls and decision steps have been identified.
☐ ☐ Potential process targets have been identified.

✓ PIP Project Sponsorship: The Work

A charter has been established.

yes no
- ☐ ☐ Charter documents work objectives and plans.
- ☐ ☐ Project-planning worksheet has been completed.
- ☐ ☐ Reporting has been established for progress and resource use.

The charter is reasonable.

yes no
- ☐ ☐ The proposed effort is feasible and consistent with overall program objectives.
- ☐ ☐ The proposed effort can be accomplished within current program constraints.
- ☐ ☐ Funding and resource needs have been identified.
- ☐ ☐ Data access and collection needs have been outlined.

✓ PIP Cause Definition: Preparation Areas

Red	Yellow	Green	Description	Comments
☐	☐	☐	**The Team** • The team has followed its authorized charter.	
☐	☐	☐	**The Improvement** • Problem definition is complete. • Causal connectedness has been established. • An initial plan for solution design has been documented.	
☐	☐	☐	**The Work** • The effort remains feasible and consistent with its initiating charter and overall program objectives.	

✓ PIP Cause Definition: The Team

The team has followed its authorized charter.

yes no
- ☐ ☐ Regular meetings have been documented.
- ☐ ☐ Participation reflects commitment.
- ☐ ☐ Any required changes have been made in team management.
- ☐ ☐ There was a clear responsibility for diagnosis.
- ☐ ☐ People responsible for diagnosis had need skills, objectivity, and time.

☑ **PIP Cause Definition: The Improvement**

Problem definition is complete.

yes no
☐ ☐ Adequate research and analysis have been completed.
☐ ☐ Analysis has identified main contributing factors.
☐ ☐ Defects were classified as individually controllable or management controllable.
☐ ☐ Pareto analysis identified the contribution of those factors to the total problem.

Causal connectedness has been established.

yes no
☐ ☐ Cause and effect analysis has identified possible causes.
☐ ☐ Data collection and analysis has isolated probable cause(s).
☐ ☐ The probable root cause of greatest impact has been identified.
☐ ☐ With high probability, causal connectedness has been established.

An initial plan for solution design has been documented.

yes no
☐ ☐ Remedy alternatives have been described.
☐ ☐ Solution approach and selection criteria have been documented.
☐ ☐ Approach is well stated in a remedy problem statement that adequately constrains the journey to follow.

☑ **PIP Cause Definition: The Work**

The effort remains feasible and consistent with overall program objectives and its initiating charter.

yes no
☐ ☐ Action plan has been documented.
☐ ☐ Action plan is reasonable.
☐ ☐ The effort can continue within current program constraints.

✓ PIP Remedy ID and Trial Ready: Preparation Areas

Red	Yellow	Green	Description	Comments
☐	☐	☐	**The Team** • The team has followed its authorized charter.	
☐	☐	☐	**The Improvement** • The remedy has been identified.	
☐	☐	☐	**The Work** • A trial plan has been documented. • The effort remains feasible and consistent with its initiating charter and overall program objectives.	

Red: ● ○ ○   Yellow: ○ ● ○   Green: ○ ○ ●

✓ PIP Remedy ID and Trial Ready: The Team

The team has followed its authorized charter.

yes no
- ☐ ☐   Regular meetings have been documented.
- ☐ ☐   Participation reflects commitment.
- ☐ ☐   Any required changes have been made in team management.

☑ **PIP Remedy ID and Trial Ready: The Improvement**

The remedy has been identified.

yes no
☐ ☐ The solution adequately addresses the problem statement.
☐ ☐ The solution is cost effective.
☐ ☐ The solution is compatible with the overall process mix.

☑ **PIP Remedy ID and Trial Ready: The Work**

A trial plan has been documented.

yes no
☐ ☐ A first application (that is, trial user) of the remedy is identified.
☐ ☐ The appropriate liaisons have been established.
☐ ☐ Schedules have been documented and reviewed.
☐ ☐ Commitment from the target organization is documented.
☐ ☐ The target organization has participated in the planning.

The effort remains feasible and consistent with overall program objectives and its initiating charter.

yes no
☐ ☐ Implementation plan has been documented.
☐ ☐ Implementation plan is reasonable.
☐ ☐ The effort can continue within current program constraints.

☑ PIP Remedy Proven: Preparation Areas

Red	Yellow	Green	Description	Comments
☐	☐	☐	**The Team** • The team has followed its authorized charter. • The trial plan has adequately been implemented.	
☐	☐	☐	**The Improvement** • Trial results support the solution. • Technology transfer issues have been adequately identified and studied.	
☐	☐	☐	**The Work** • A realistic transition plan has been documented.	

☑ PIP Remedy Proven: The Team

The team has followed its authorized charter.

yes no
- ☐ ☐ Regular meetings have been documented.
- ☐ ☐ Participation reflects commitment.
- ☐ ☐ Any required changes have been made in team management.

The trial plan has been adequately implemented.

yes no
- ☐ ☐ The trial results have been documented.
- ☐ ☐ The trial proceeded according to plan, with exceptions noted.

☑ **PIP Remedy Proven: The Improvement**

Trial results support the solution.

yes no
☐ ☐   Adequate remedy trial has been completed.
☐ ☐   The remedy adequately addresses the root cause of the stated problem.
☐ ☐   The remedy is cost effective.
☐ ☐   The remedy is compatible with the overall process mix.

Technology transfer issues have been adequately identified and studied.

yes no
☐ ☐   The solution can be transitioned to general use.
☐ ☐   Training has been made available.
☐ ☐   Difficulties have been discussed and documented.

☑ **PIP Remedy Proven: The Work**

A realistic transition plan has been documented.

yes no
☐ ☐   Action plans address roadblocks.
☐ ☐   Maintenance plans or plans for continued monitoring and reporting have been documented.

✓	**PIP Remedy Transitioned: Preparation Areas**	

Red	Yellow	Green	Description	Comments
☐	☐	☐	**The Team** • The team has followed its authorized charter. • The transition plan was successfully executed.	
☐	☐	☐	**The Improvement** • The solution has proven effective in general use.	
☐	☐	☐	**The Work** • Any further controls, as necessary, have been planned. • Recommendations have been provided for further application or refinement.	

☑ **PIP Remedy Transitioned: The Team**

The team has followed its authorized charter.

yes no
☐ ☐ Regular meetings have been documented.
☐ ☐ Participation reflects commitment.
☐ ☐ Any required changes have been made in team management.

The transition plan was successfully executed.

yes no
☐ ☐ Transition process deficiencies have been identified and corrected where possible.
☐ ☐ Work-arounds or alternatives have been documented for transition process deficiencies.
☐ ☐ Transition proceeded according to plan, with exceptions noted.
☐ ☐ A postmortem view of the remedy, the process improvement process, and its phases have been documented.

☑ **PIP Remedy Transitioned: The Improvement**

The solution has proven effective in general use.

yes no
☐ ☐ Root causes have visibly been affected.
☐ ☐ Solution effectiveness is supported by data collected.
☐ ☐ The solution is an integral part of the overall process mix.
☐ ☐ Any immediate corrective action was approved, implemented, and verified effective.
☐ ☐ A new level of performance was achieved by removing root causes.

☑ PIP Remedy Transitioned: The Work

Any further controls, as necessary, have been planned.

yes no
☐ ☐ A tracking system has been planned to provide continued results reporting.
☐ ☐ Audits, or some other mechanism(s), have been defined to ensure the consistency of process execution.

Recommendations have been provided for further application or refinement.

yes no
☐ ☐ These include suggestions addressing the process improvement program (PIP).
☐ ☐ These include suggestions addressing execution of the PIP.
☐ ☐ These include suggestions addressing fine-tuning or evolving the remedy.
☐ ☐ These include suggestions for providing further PIP candidates.

PROCESS CHECKLISTS

☑ **Common Process Concerns**

yes   no

☐   ☐   A taxonomy for standards exists.
☐   ☐   The process (in question) is well defined.
☐   ☐   Expectations for the process are understood and its position within the taxonomy is appropriate.
☐   ☐   Training plans or programs exist that address curricula, courses, budgets, intended audience, schedules, and sources for materials and trainers.
☐   ☐   Training exists on the related topics of group dynamics and interpersonal effectiveness.
☐   ☐   A mechanism exists (e.g., in-process audits) to meter and ensure consistent process application.
☐   ☐   A feedback mechanism exists to inform participants of the value of their participation, the value of the object of the process (e.g., the deliverable reviewed, the baseline audited, or the project reviewed), and the value of the process itself (i.e., whether process expectations were met).
☐   ☐   The company's reward system is attuned to process objectives.
☐   ☐   Execution of the process does not adversely affect individual performance appraisals.

✓ Product Review Implementation

yes no

☐ ☐ Time for applying the review process(es) is scheduled into the overall project plan.

☐ ☐ Participation will have a positive effect on individual merit ratings.

☐ ☐ The review results will *not* affect individual merit ratings, either positively or negatively.

☐ ☐ Review participation is required of, but not limited to, people representing functional responsibilities as identified in a "required reviewer matrix."

☐ ☐ Moderator/leader training is available.

☐ ☐ Adequate coordination or facilitator support is provided.

☐ ☐ Related standards are reviewed and improvements planned (e.g., standard documentation formats to improve ease of review and review coverage consistency) to support the review processes.

☐ ☐ The standards, forms, support, data collection schemes, required attendance, report distribution, etc. relating to the review process have all been reviewed.

☑ Project Review Implementation

yes no

☐ ☐ Policy requires review application. Any exceptions to the policy are documented.

☐ ☐ The review process is defined in program-level standards. Application requirements are also defined.

☐ ☐ The review provides a decision-making mechanism with the "profit and loss" manager and key players in attendance, or with the key players acting with the delegated authority of that manager.

☐ ☐ The difference between process execution and management prerogative is understood. The process provides the appraisal and valuation. Authority can be used to make a documented business decision contrary to that appraisal.

☐ ☐ The "profit and loss" manager is accountable for any deviation from recommended practice or outcome contrary to the review.

☐ ☐ Meeting ownership is both clear and exercised.

☐ ☐ Application of the review process is scheduled into the overall project plan as a major event and project disposition after the review, when passed, is a major milestone.

☐ ☐ Standard entry and exit criteria exist for each project review.

☐ ☐ Development standards provide for consistent product format and content as well as define acceptance criteria.

☐ ☐ The project issues to be reviewed are identified in program-level standards.

☐ ☐ The appropriate organizational elements are represented at all project reviews.

☐ ☐ Success criteria are known in advance of the review.

☐ ☐ The standards, forms, support, data collection schemes, required attendance, report distribution, etc. relating to the review process have all been reviewed.

✓ Audit Implementation

yes no

☐ ☐ Objective audit criteria exist.
☐ ☐ Audit personnel are selected to promote team objectivity.
☐ ☐ Audit personnel are given sufficient authority by appropriate management to perform the audit.
☐ ☐ The auditing organization develops and follows an audit plan for each audit performed.
☐ ☐ The auditing organization follows its own reasonable and prudent procedures. It is not the last bastion of unstructuredness telling the rest of the world how structured it should be.
☐ ☐ The audit team understands the organization to be audited.
☐ ☐ The audit team understands the products and processes.
☐ ☐ The audit team understands the objective audit criteria to be used.
☐ ☐ The audit program (and the plan for each audit) is designed to minimize disruption.
☐ ☐ The audit program includes quality program, in-process, and configuration audits.
☐ ☐ The audit program includes vendor audits as appropriate.
☐ ☐ The auditing organization is independent of any organizations audited.
☐ ☐ Any audit recommendations are reported separately from results.
☐ ☐ Audit results document objective, verifiable statements.

PRODUCT CHECKLISTS

✓	**General Document Requirements**

yes no
- ☐ ☐ The document has a unique (and correct) identifier prominently displayed.
- ☐ ☐ The document is complete.
- ☐ ☐ The document is internally consistent.
- ☐ ☐ The document is unambiguous.
- ☐ ☐ Its contents are appropriate and correct.
- ☐ ☐ All assumptions that have been made are well documented.
- ☐ ☐ Acronyms are expanded and special terms are defined.
- ☐ ☐ It has adequate references to Governing Documents (i.e., standards or plans).
- ☐ ☐ It has adequate references to Parent Documents (e.g., the High Level Design for a Low Level Design Document).
- ☐ ☐ It has adequate references to Supporting Documents (e.g., journal papers or internal memoranda to support algorithms, describe the methodology used, or other background).
- ☐ ☐ Distribution list is appropriate and up to date, identifying recipient, function (as function may outlive the person who performs it), and location.
- ☐ ☐ Approval and signature blocks are appropriate.
- ☐ ☐ Document release version, revision level, disposition (i.e., draft, final, and so on), date, author, and owner (administrator) are prominently displayed.
- ☐ ☐ Proprietary markings are prominent, appropriate, and reflect a reasonable level of caution. Declassification date is also identified.

☑ Requirements Documentation

yes no

- ☐ ☐ The Requirements Specification Document complies to standards and is consistent with recommended practice. See general checklist for documents.
- ☐ ☐ Traceability exists from the next higher-level specification (e.g., system specification or user requirements specification).
- ☐ ☐ External interfaces (e.g., hardware, firmware or other systems) are compatible.
- ☐ ☐ The requirements for the man-machine interface are adequate.
- ☐ ☐ Feasibility has adequately been defended.
- ☐ ☐ Required Performance is specified for Response.
- ☐ ☐ Required Performance is specified for Capacity.
- ☐ ☐ Required Performance is specified for Quantity.
- ☐ ☐ Required Performance is specified for Accuracy.
- ☐ ☐ Required Performance is specified for Reliability.
- ☐ ☐ Protocols are specified for I/O messages.
- ☐ ☐ Protocols are specified for Signaling.
- ☐ ☐ Requirements are verifiable by test or other studies.
- ☐ ☐ Operational test cases can be derived.
- ☐ ☐ All failure modes and responses are specified for operation under engineered conditions.
- ☐ ☐ All failure modes and responses are specified for resource failure conditions.
- ☐ ☐ All needed measurements have been specified for engineering.
- ☐ ☐ Requirements do not restrict the design.
- ☐ ☐ Desired relationship with existing and planned functionality is specified.

☑ **Common Design Document Issues**

yes	no	
☐	☐	The Design Document complies to standards and is consistent with recommended practice. See general checklist for documents.
☐	☐	It is a natural extension of its parent document. They are consistent.
☐	☐	The design/representation methodology is stated and followed.
☐	☐	The design is consistent with existing data structures.
☐	☐	Any modification to global data structures or values (including further restrictions) have been clearly documented (and approved!).
☐	☐	The design is consistent with the system architecture.
☐	☐	Memory requirements are specified.
☐	☐	Data structures are understandable (maintainable), meaningful, and auditable.
☐	☐	Data value ranges are specified wherever appropriate.
☐	☐	Data values to be set by customer/user are identified, modifiable, and documented for the user.
☐	☐	Recording capabilities are achievable as required for event-driven data collection.
☐	☐	User interfaces (e.g., terminal commands, responses, forms, menus) are fully specified.
☐	☐	The error handling scenario is complete and appropriate.
☐	☐	Error messages are meaningful to the user, well documented, and managed as a set to avoid inconsistency, ambiguity, gaps, or redundancies.
☐	☐	All interfaces with other systems/subsystems are complete, correct, clean, and well defined.
☐	☐	Interfaces follow required/recommended practice for coupling, cohesion, format, sequence, and so on.
☐	☐	Complexity has been minimized.

✓ Architectural Design Document

Accuracy

yes	no	
☐	☐	Accuracy requirements are met by the numerical techniques associated with algorithms being used.
☐	☐	Any library routines that are planned for use meet accuracy requirements.
☐	☐	The data base allows, by design, adequate space for accuracy requirements.

Completeness

☐	☐	The design adequately defines inputs, processing, databases, and outputs.
☐	☐	Traceability back to the requirements is evident for functional requirements.
☐	☐	Traceability back to the requirements is evident for fault tolerance requirements.
☐	☐	Traceability back to the requirements is evident for performance requirements.
☐	☐	Traceability back to the requirements is evident for security requirements.
☐	☐	Traceability back to the requirements is evident for safety requirements.
☐	☐	Traceability back to the requirements is evident for interface requirements.
☐	☐	The architecture of the program is clearly depicted and elements are properly allocated to subordinate levels of design.

Interfaces and I/O

☐	☐	Any user-provided inputs and are designed with that user in mind.
☐	☐	Input is terminated with a well defined and logical "end of input."
☐	☐	Guidance is available and input can be verified by the user before execution.
☐	☐	Input error messages are clear and informative.
☐	☐	Any output options are clear and easy to use.
☐	☐	Any optional outputs are designed with the user in mind.
☐	☐	The relationship between error messages and outputs is clear.
☐	☐	The interfaces with all other subsystems are well defined and adequate.

Modularity

☐	☐	Module invocation falls within limits and module sizes fall within limits.
☐	☐	Modules perform single functions that are readily mapped to requirements.
☐	☐	Module state is refreshed after execution and failure, as appropriate.

☑ Detailed Design Documentation

Consistency and Completeness

yes no
- ☐ ☐ Design is consistent with the design of other modules.
- ☐ ☐ The module design adequately addresses all design issues identified and deferred in the architectural design specification.
- ☐ ☐ The design is adequately portrayed and is not ambiguous.
- ☐ ☐ Interfaces with other modules/externals are well defined and adequate.
- ☐ ☐ Design of interfaces is consistent in communicating modules.
- ☐ ☐ Input handling is consistent with origin of input.
- ☐ ☐ Output handling is consistent with receptor of output.
- ☐ ☐ Data base handling is consistent with data base conventions.
- ☐ ☐ Data are available (e.g., logic diagrams, algorithms, storage allocation charts, flow charts, PDL) to establish design integrity and requirements traceability.
- ☐ ☐ Statement of function flow, timing, sizing, storage requirements, memory maps, data base interaction, and other parameters related to performance.
- ☐ ☐ Typical use scenarios have been refined for user interaction with critical functions.
- ☐ ☐ Performance goals have been refined for each scenario.

Error Handling
- ☐ ☐ The module is designed to perform checks on all error conditions.
- ☐ ☐ Inputs are validated for type and range.
- ☐ ☐ Conflicting inputs are identified and an opportunity is provided to back out.
- ☐ ☐ Errors are blocked on input or reported before processing.
- ☐ ☐ Error messages are adequate, timely, consistently applied, and complete.
- ☐ ☐ Automatic error correction is provided, and warnings issued, as appropriate.

Modularity
- ☐ ☐ The module is designed within size limits.
- ☐ ☐ The module is designed within complexity limits.
- ☐ ☐ The module has single entry and exit points.
- ☐ ☐ Module interfaces are kept to a minimum.

✓		**Code**
yes	**no**	
☐	☐	The code is adequately and correctly documented.
☐	☐	Any required frontal documentation (i.e., "prolog") or documentation file is adequately provided.
☐	☐	The code follows applicable standards for structure, style, naming conventions, portability, and so on.
☐	☐	The code provides appropriate tests for input or parameter validity and plausibility.
☐	☐	All code is executable (can be reached) and logic is consistent and correct.
☐	☐	The program and all of its loops will terminate.
☐	☐	Algorithms are complete and correct.
☐	☐	Variables are uniquely named and defined before use.
☐	☐	Initialization is complete and correct.
☐	☐	Variable names are not sensitive to the possibility of compiler or loader truncation.
☐	☐	All external variables and data structures are declared.
☐	☐	All allowable variable values (including zero ?) are within range.
☐	☐	Interrupts, user, operator precedences, etc., are obvious.
☐	☐	The possibility of intermediate data results (e.g., underflow or overflow) has been checked and resolved.
☐	☐	All mixed-mode computations and comparisons have been checked. This includes assignment of variables with different width.
☐	☐	The code satisfies the design it implements.
☐	☐	The code is maintainable.
☐	☐	Documentation agrees with the implementation.

☑ Common Test Plan Issues

Environment
yes no
- ☐ ☐ Necessary and desired properties of the test environment have been specified using physical characteristics, the mode of use (e.g., stand-alone), and so on. Availability is stated.
- ☐ ☐ Any special test tool or other testing needs (e.g., office space) have been described and the source for those unavailable has been identified.

Logistics
yes no
- ☐ ☐ Transmittal media characteristics pertinent to testing are discussed (e.g., programs that need to be transferred from tape to disk).
- ☐ ☐ The testing constraints (e.g., test resource availability) have been identified.
- ☐ ☐ Required staffing has been identified by skill level, and training options have been presented to provide the appropriate skill levels.
- ☐ ☐ High risk assumptions (e.g., timely delivery of critical third-party test hardware) and contingency plans for each are stated.

Test Documents
yes no
- ☐ ☐ The test document complies to standards and is consistent with recommended practice. See general checklist for documents.
- ☐ ☐ References include Requirements Specification, Design Specifications of the appropriate abstraction, Users Guide, Operations Guide, Installation Guide.

Test Items
yes no
- ☐ ☐ Test items, along with their version and revision levels, are clearly identified.
- ☐ ☐ All software features (and combinations of software features) to be tested have been identified, as has the test-design specification for each.
- ☐ ☐ All software features (and combinations of software features) not to be tested are identified, the reasoning documented, and the risks estimated.
- ☐ ☐ Active incident reports relating to test items should be identified, as should any items excluded from testing.

☑ Common Test Plan Issues (cont.)

Activities

yes no

☐ ☐ The testing approach is described in such detail as to allow identification of the major testing tasks and associated time requirements.

☐ ☐ The comprehensiveness of the testing effort has been identified (e.g., error frequency and execution coverage requirements).

☐ ☐ The set of tasks needed to prepare for and perform testing has been identified, along with any interdependencies and special resources or skills required.

☐ ☐ The test effort, as appropriate, adequately provides for stress, load, recovery, security, regression, interface, functional, and performance testing.

☐ ☐ Responsibilities have been identified for who is to deliver the test items, manage, design tests, prepare the lab, execute the tests, witness the tests, check results, and resolve issues.

☐ ☐ Criteria have been documented for use in determining whether to suspend (and resume) any or all testing activity associated with the test plan. Activities to be repeated on resuming have also been stated.

☐ ☐ Milestones are clearly stated. Those that are printed in the Software Project Management Document are repeated. Item transmittal events are included. The schedule is specified for each major task and its completion date, resources used, and their period of use.

Outputs

yes no

☐ ☐ Criteria have been documented for use in determining whether each test item has passed or failed testing.

☐ ☐ The deliverable documents have been identified, including and test I/O data.

☐ ☐ A test coverage matrix maps tests to requirements including functional and performance requirements. The mapping shows adequate coverage.

☐ ☐ Wherever test item evaluation did not proceed according to plan, the situation is documented. Test items that could not be tested and those that experienced attenuated testing are identified with contingencies and risks stated.

☑ Test Specifications

Test-Design Specification

yes no

☐ ☐ All software features to be tested have been identified and include a reference to their associated requirements.
☐ ☐ Changes to the test plan approach have been stated.
☐ ☐ Testing techniques and methods of analysis have been identified.
☐ ☐ Pass/fail criteria have been stated.
☐ ☐ The need for each test case has been established and requirements have been set.

Test-Case Specification

yes no

☐ ☐ Test items and features addressed by the specification have been identified.
☐ ☐ Inputs and outputs required to execute the test case have been identified.
☐ ☐ Hardware and software requirements have been identified. Included are any special training requirements or special facilities needed.
☐ ☐ Special procedures (e.g., setup, operation, or intervention) have been identified.
☐ ☐ Dependencies on other test cases have been identified.

Test-Procedure Specification

yes no

☐ ☐ References to related test-design specifications and test cases have been stated.
☐ ☐ Execution steps have been identified (e.g., setup, start, terminate/restart, stop, or measure).

✓ Test Reports and Records

Test Item Transmittal Report

yes no

☐ ☐ Test items to be transmitted have been described. Included are references to the related test plan and the people responsible for the test item.

☐ ☐ The media containing the test items is identified.

☐ ☐ Test item status has been described. Included are deviations from the test plan, documentation changes pending, and trouble reports resolved by the item.

☐ ☐ Approvals for transmission have been obtained.

Test Log

☐ ☐ Items tested are identified.

☐ ☐ Test environment is described.

☐ ☐ Entry contains date and time.

☐ ☐ People present have been noted.

☐ ☐ Hardware and software anomalies have been described (e.g., power failure and failure of test procedure to execute) both before and after the failure.

Test Incident Report

☐ ☐ Incident summary includes reference to test procedures or test-case specifications.

☐ ☐ The incident has been described in detail. Included is all information needed to isolate/duplicate the incident (e.g., inputs, expected results, environment, procedure, or attempts to repeat).

☐ ☐ Impact of incident is clearly described.

Test Summary Report

☐ ☐ The testing environment has been described and resource use has been noted.

☐ ☐ Item references have been provided.

☐ ☐ Variations between item and reference (e.g., design, test plan, or test procedure) have been noted.

☐ ☐ Features not fully tested as required by the test plan have been identified and details of that test inadequacy have been related.

☐ ☐ Both resolved and unresolved incidents have been described.

☐ ☐ Test item pass/fail evaluation has been noted and supported.

APPENDIX 2

Sample Forms

Forms can help you get and stay organized in your quest for information. The first two forms provided are in support of the auditing process. Specifically, the first helps in gathering information during an interview session and the second establishes a feedback path from the interviewee after the session. The interview worksheet is relatively straightforward with the exception of the "issues" and "verifiable statements" sections. Issues are either those fundamental questions chosen specifically for the interviewee from checklists and other sources before the interview, or issues identified during the interview as a result of the dialog you establish. Verifiable statements are statements that have existed as issues but that, as a result of the current dialog, are considered to have been verified. These can include statements that have been heard from multiple sources, or statements that originate with an individual who is considered the subject matter owner or expert.

The next two forms support project reviews for product realization, and both a milestone declaration and product release authorization forms are provided. Also in this section are two forms that support project reviews for process improvement: the project authorization request and the progress record.

Inspections are then supported by various forms that are used as part of the inspection process. These include the inspection meeting notice, the discussion items list, and the inspection report form. The discussion items list gets its name from the particular approach taken in identifying and recording defects. With this example, the inspection team has the option of identifying possible problems with the parent document or product specification against which the current product is examined. Thus, the form represents more than just a defect list. Identifying a potential problem in the parent would result in a defect type of "P: Possible misdirection" being recorded. Any and all inconsistencies with the parent are still recorded against the current product as defects.

As with the checklists, all forms are provided as a starting point for your redesign or editing.

AUDIT FORMS

Interview Worksheet				
Interviewee		Org/Location		Telephone
Meeting Date	Time		Place	Reference Number
Group _____ Group Function			Related Areas/Follow-up	
Interviewee Function				
Issues			Verifiable Statements	

Interview Feedback			
Interviewee	**Org/Location**		**Telephone**
Meeting Date	**Time**	**Place**	

What is your general reaction to this audit? To the interview?

Were there any questions that were awkward or uncomfortable to answer?

Were there any questions that you wish you had answered better?

Was there anything that you said, on reflection, that you wish you hadn't? Anything to add?

What can the interview team do to improve? Were they cooperative?

Do you have any other comments or concerns?

PROJECT REVIEW FORMS

Project Milestone Declaration				
Project		**Product Line**	**Product Identifiers**	
Date	**Product Line Manager**	**Project Manager**	**Quality Engineer**	

Milestone Met:

As Evidenced By:

Open Items	Responsibility	Action Plans

Signatures:

Product Release Authorization		
Product	**Configuration Identifiers**	**Champion**
Date		

Open Items   **Responsibility**   **Action Plans**

Signatures:

Improvement Project Authorization Request

Chair	Co-Chair	Secretary
Date of Application	**Date of Decision**	**Decision**	**P A R Number**

Initial Team Members	Organization	Location	Phone

Project Description (attachments as needed)

Approval Board Signatures

Improvement Project Progress Record

Chair	Co-Chair	Secretary	
Date of Application	Date of Approval	Date of Completion	P A R Number

Initial Team Members	Organization	Location	Phone

Final Team Members	Organization	Location	Phone

Brief Project Description

Progress Log

Review or Event	Outcome	Comments	Plans

174 SAMPLE FORMS

INSPECTION FORMS

INSPECTION MEETING NOTICE						
Inspection Meeting							
Moderator:				Producer:		
Date(s):		Time(s):			Location(s):	
Inspection Type (Check One)							
Project Planning		*Development*			*Testing*	
☐ Development		☐ Requirements			*Plans*	
☐ SQA		☐ Architecture			☐ System	
☐ Project Mgt		☐ Detailed Design			☐ Feature/Subsystem	
☐ Configuration Mgt		☐ Arch/Detail Design			☐ Integration	
☐ V&V		☐ Code			☐ Unit	
☐		*Enhancement/Major Fix*			*Specifications*	
☐		☐ *Design*			☐ Test Design	
☐		☐ *Code*			☐ Test Procedure	
☐		☐ *Test*			☐ Test Case	
☐ *Other* (Specify below)		☐ *Other* (Specify below)			☐ *Other* (Specify below)	
Product to be Inspected							
Release Stream	Tracking Identifier	Work Brkdn Structure ID	DESCRIPTION	Materials			
				Date Distributed		Product Size
Inspection Number (initial, first reinspection, et cetera): _____							
Inspection Participation						See Required Reviewer Matrix	
Role	*Name, Dept, Location, Phone*				*Represented Viewpoint*	
Moderator:						
Reader:						
Recorder:						
Author:					Product Ownership	
Other Team Members						

DISCUSSION ITEMS LIST

Product to be Inspected

Release Stream	Tracking Identifier	Work Brkdn Structure ID	DESCRIPTION	Materials Date Distributed	Product Size

Inspection Number (initial, first reinspection, et cetera): _____

Inspection Type (Check One)

Project Planning	Development	Testing
☐ Development	☐ Requirements	*Plans*
☐ SQA	☐ Architecture	☐ System
☐ Project Mgt	☐ Detailed Design	☐ Feature/Subsystem
☐ Configuration Mgt	☐ Arch/Detail Design	☐ Integration
☐ V&V	☐ Code	☐ Unit
☐	*Enhancement/Major Fix*	*Specifications*
☐	☐ Design	☐ Test Design
☐	☐ Code	☐ Test Procedure
☐	☐ Test	☐ Test Case
☐ Other (Specify below)	☐ Other (Specify below)	☐ Other (Specify below)

DEFECT CLASSIFICATION (Check Type, Severity, & Category)

Defect Type	Defect Severity	Category (cont.)
M: Missing	1: Major	LO: Logic
W: Wrong	2: Minor	PE: Performance
E: Extra		SC: Stds Compliance
P: Possible Misdirection	Defect Category	WF: Writing Format
(that is, product consistent	CO: Computation	WG: Grammar, et cetera
with specification or Parent,	DA: Data Handling	AM: Ambiguous
BUT a defect may exist in	HW: Hardware	
Parent) Ignore categories when	FW: Firmware	
possible misdirection exists.	IF: Interface	OT: Other

Use copies of page 2 to record specific defects. Use the classification scheme shown above.

DISCUSSION ITEMS LIST (Continued)

Item #	Type	Severity	Cat.	Description	Additional info source

Inspection Report Form

Product Inspected

Release Stream	Tracking Identifier	Work Brkdn Structure ID	DESCRIPTION	Product Size

Inspection Number (initial, first reinspection, et cetera):   Estimated Rework:

Inspection Process

Inspection Date	Meeting Duration	Distribution Date	Reading Method:
			☐ Line-by-line ☐ Paraphrasing ☐ Mix

Product Disposition

☐ Accept as Noted   ☐ Rework with Moderator Verification   ☐ Rework and Re-inspect

Participant SIGN-OFF

Role	INIT	Name	Suggested Disp	Represented Viewpoint	Prep Time	Experience (1–5) Viewpoint	Product
Moderator:							
Reader:							
Recorder:							
Author:			N/A	Product Ownership			5
Others:							

REWORK VERIFICATION (required for Dispositions 2 and 3)

Time Expended Author Rework	Moderator Verification	Date Verified	Moderator Initials	Moderator Name, Dept, Loc, Ext.

Items remaining open on verification include:

Original # from list	Description	Why still open	Assignment

APPENDIX 3

SAMPLE LETTERS

Letter writing is perhaps one of the most difficult parts of auditing. To help start your auditing program, five key letters have been provided as a starting point for your editing. Although attuned to a particular style of software quality program auditing, they can still be used as a model for other audit types. These letters include an SQPA announcement that can double as a cover for the audit plan, a preparation letter, a cover letter for reviewing the results report, a cover letter for delivery of the results report, and a cover letter for the delivery of recommendations.

MEMORANDUM [DATE]

To: Management of [Audited Organization]
From: Audit Supervisor
Subject: Software Quality Program Audit ANNOUNCEMENT

This memo is to inform you that a Software Quality Program Audit (SQPA) is being planned for [Audited Organization/Projects], and will be managed by YYY. This audit is driven by .... , as well as a request from ..... Specifically, [Auditing Organization] will perform an SQPA to ensure that [Audited Organization/Projects] is subject to an effective Software Quality Program by determining:

- How well the software quality program documentation addresses the basic elements of Software Quality Assurance.
- How well the [Audited Organization/Projects] organizations follow their formal program.

Findings (the audit results) will be reported separately from recommendations. Statements in the results report will be objective and verifiable. The results report will be reviewed for accuracy by some of your key people. Specific recommendations based on these documented results (and on various business factors) will then be published by [Auditing Organization].

The scope of the audit covers all [Audited Organization/Projects] activities based in [Locations] and those interface mechanisms and liaisons with other locations. This involves reviewing project documentation, interviewing key personnel, and examining selected project activities.

A formal audit plan is to be completed (with the assistance of the local director of quality) to identify specific audit activities, report format and distribution, and those individuals within your organization to act as key contacts for documentation collection, identification of activities to be observed, and interview planning.

These activities are being planned so as to minimize interference with your already numerous and important efforts.

Regards,

Charles P. Hollocker
Copy to: Management of [Auditing Organization]

MEMORANDUM [DATE]

To: All Potential Interviewees
From: Lead Auditor
Subject: Software Quality Program Audit PREPARATION

During [time period] [the auditing organization] will perform a Software Quality Program Audit of [AUDITED ORGANIZATION, LOCATION]. The purpose of the audit is to determine how well the current software quality program documentation addresses the basic elements of Software Quality Assurance and how well your formal program is followed.

The scope of this Audit covers the activities of [AUDITED ORGANIZATION, LOCATION] and their liaisons. The audit is driven by a formal plan and will provide three reports:

- **The Results Report:** This is the documented results of having (1) examined current documentation, (2) interviewed selected staff members, and (3) made other project observations. The Results Report will be objective, verifiable, and will contain no recommendations or other subjective expression of opinion. The Results Report is published by [the auditing organization] after review by the audited organization.
- **The Recommendations Report:** This is the formal presentation of recommendations to your management. Recommendations are based on audit results, the business environment, and the past experiences and subjective judgments of the audit team. It is left to the recipients of this report to collaborate in decisions establishing priorities, and to chart a course of action. Recommendations are published (and response requested) by [the auditing organization].
- **The Executive Summary:** Although there is a need to limit the ascent of unnecessary detail, a brief summary of audit activities, including an overview of recommendations, will be published by [the auditing organization].

Four general methods of information gathering are used in the SQPA:

- Examination of process documentation
- Examination of selected in-process products
- Interview of staff
- Process witnessing

Key audit contacts (people from your own project) will be informed regularly of audit progress. Moreover, these contacts will regularly desk check the results report as it is being developed and participate in a formal review of the final draft. Their participation in verifying report accuracy is critical to audit success.

Quality Program Documentation will be examined for (1) coverage, (2) consistency and uniformity of purpose, and (3) adequacy. To reduce unwanted subjectivity and to find some meter for comparison, the *ANSI/IEEE Standard for Software Quality Assurance Plans* (ANSI/IEEE Std 730-1984) has been selected as representing reasonable and prudent coverage for documentation of this type.

The audit team will request specific documentation on initiating the audit. All documents considered in the program documentation analysis will be identified in the results report.

Availability of interviewees is important to audit success. Also, audit team attendance at meetings, tour of facilities, and witnessing of specific project activities (that is, witnessing verification testing) is an important part of determining how the Software Quality Program is executed.

Members of the [AUDITED ORGANIZATION] management team are requested to:

- Provide facilities and services in support of the audit (that is, office, phone, locking file cabinet, and secretary).
- Formally react to audit recommendations by issuing a memo describing, in general terms, what actions are to be initiated as a result of those recommendations. Any unacceptable recommendations will be identified and your position stated in adequate detail as to show the recommendation inappropriate.

Key contacts, being a crucial information source and an audit partner, will work closely with the audit team to assist them in:

- Receiving needed quality program documentation
- Establishing interview schedules and selecting people to interview
- Coordinating process witnessing and selecting candidate activities
- Reviewing the audit progress and results report to assure accurate representation

Key contacts should ensure that their phones will be answered. Key contacts may also be interviewees.

Recommendations cited by the audit team will be documented along with your organization's response. Improvement projects will be tracked and monitored by your organization with periodic status reports required by [the auditing organization] Services. Your organization will need your cooperation and active participation to achieve problem resolution. Details of those activities are, of course, the responsibility of your management.

Because the audit team will need time to digest what they learn, interviews will probably occur in two or three blocks of three days each. Each interview will be scheduled to last 30 minutes. Some interviews may only be to follow up on issues from earlier interviews, so some sessions may be shorter and you might be called back for further consultation on a specific issue.

You are a key part of the audit activity. Honest response to questions and a cooperative attitude is expected from you, and the audit team likewise owes you the courtesy of confidentiality. If you have documents that you feel are representative of your function's work or that define your function, please bring them to the interview or identify them for the audit team. This will speed resolution of inconsistencies that might appear in the audit results.

Other points of interest include:

- All interviews will be held away from your office. The audit team will try to give you at least a week's notice.
- You are the recognized expert when it comes to your specific assignment, and you will be treated with respect.
- Newer employees should identify themselves and know their training program.
- If a question is confusing, you should ask to have it repeated or rephrased. Do not be afraid to ask the audit team questions.
- Do not deliberately mislead or falsify information.
- Do not answer questions outside of your area of responsibility and expertise.
- Emphasize the strong points of your job.
- Do not forget to fill out the post interview form and return it to the audit team's secretary. It should only take a moment and might alleviate the need to ask you to a follow-up interview.

You might expect certain questions:

- To start with, the audit team will probably ask you to give an overview of your team's responsibilities followed by your own responsibilities.
- The audit team is concerned about standards, practices, reports and other documents, and about how accuracy is ensured.
- How does work flow from one group or individual to the next step? Who is your customer? How do individual functions relate to the entire project?
- The audit team frequently asks about problem reporting and corrective action procedures covering both product and process problems.
- Distribution, usefulness, and frequency of publication are all important quality report issues.
- Be prepared to discuss your involvement in any quality or productivity improvement programs (for example, quality circles or special projects).

These activities are being planned so as to minimize interference with your already numerous and important efforts. Please call us at [number] with any questions or suggestions, as we would like you to work out any concerns in advance of your interview.

Regards,

Charles P. Hollocker

MEMORANDUM [DATE]

To: Key Contacts, Interviewees, and Supervision of [Audited Org.]
From: Audit supervisor
Subject: Review of Audit Results

    You have been an important part of the audit effort. After examining quality program documentation and observing your program in progress, the audit team has produced a detailed results report in draft form. Having a reasonable and prudent quality program that is well documented and evenly applied is of extreme importance.
    We ask further assistance toward achieving this goal. Before any report is finalized, as further assurance that our findings are accurate, we ask that you spend an hour or two reviewing the attached draft and use copies of the attached form to document your feedback. Form use is important because we want to show how serious we are about responding to your valuable feedback, and to track changes to the results draft.
    Please provide feedback within a week of receiving this letter. We will return copies of feedback, indicating our corrective action, to their originator.
    Key contacts from your organization have been working with us to establish this final draft. Their review of the previous draft(s) is appreciated.

Regards,

Charles P. Hollocker

Att. (as stated)

MEMORANDUM [DATE]

To:
From:
Subject: Delivery of Audit Results

This package provides the final audit results document for the audit recently performed by [Auditing Organization, (Location)]. The cooperation and support received from you and your people were greatly appreciated.

Within your organization, supervisory contacts for this audit have already received earlier drafts of these results and their comments have been incorporated.

This results document will be followed by a separately issued recommendations report. An executive summary of the audit, including an overview of recommendations, will be issued to [Upper Management].

Regards,

Charles P. Hollocker

Att. (as stated)
Copy (with att.) to:

MEMORANDUM [DATE]

To:
From:
Subject: Post-audit Recommendations

   With this package, [Auditing Organization (Location)] delivers its recommendations to management responsible for [Audited Organization/Project]. As you already know, this audit followed a formal plan involving the cooperation and support of people in your organization.
   Please share these recommendations with your subordinates. To avoid imposing on your responsibilities, we do not impose priorities with these recommendations. We do however, require a formal (single) response to inform us, in general terms, of process changes you intend to implement.
   We ask for this response within a month of this letter's date. We in [Auditing Organization], are eager to extend an offer of consultation to your organization to assist in charting a course of action, or simply to clarify our recommendations. An executive summary of the audit activity, including an overview of recommendations, will be issued to [Upper Management].

Regards,

Charles P. Hollocker

Att. (as stated)
Copy (with att.) to:

APPENDIX 4
PLANS AND REPORTS

Similar to letter writing, the generation of plans and reports can be a concern people can burn countless hours discussing. Examples have been provided here for both audits and reviews. The SQPA was again chosen as the subject matter for the auditing documents. This provides both consistency with other elements of the handbook and an opportunity to start with (and pare down) the auditing activity that provides the greatest scope. Also included in this package is a test verification report (TVR) skeleton that may be needed if your audit includes having your team perform any testing first hand. Because a TVR has broader applications than audits, the report is presented in a somewhat generalized form.

To support your review program, two reports have been provided as a starting point for your editing. Although they reflect use of the inspection process, they can still be used as a model for other review types. These reports provide a weekly and monthly summary of some common review data.

AUDIT PLANS AND REPORTS

AUDIT PLAN

Software Quality Program Audit for

[THE AUDITED ORGANIZATION]

1. INTRODUCTION

During [month(s), year], [the auditing organization] will perform a Software Quality Program Audit of [THE AUDITED ORGANIZATION, LOCATION].

The purpose of the audit is to ensure that [THE AUDITED ORGANIZATION] is subject to an effective Software Quality Program. This activity will proceed with two major objectives:

- Determine how well the software quality program documentation addresses the basic elements of Software Quality Assurance.
- Determine how well the [THE AUDITED ORGANIZATION] follows its formal program.

1.1 Audit Scope

The scope of this audit covers the [THE AUDITED ORGANIZATION, LOCATION] and their liaisons. There are, however, certain scope restrictions. Specifically, _____ .

The audit team will work very closely with [THE AUDITED ORGANIZATION] management and personnel to manage audit team interactions with the organization and to minimize interference with their regular activities.

1.2 Report Description and Distribution

Because this is an effort exemplary of [THE AUDITED ORGANIZATION] management's commitment to process improvement, detailed reports will not be widely distributed.

1.2.1 The Audit Plan

A complete, concise, and well executed plan is crucial to successful audit completion. A successful audit is one where: (1) Results accurately portray the true program state, (2) Recommendations are both possible and appropriate, and (3) Recipients of the report have confidence in the report and a willingness to respond to the recommendations. The Audit Plan is published by [the auditing organization] after review by the audited organization and executive support. Planned recipients, by responsibility are:

Responsibility	Name	Location
VP of Operations		
VP of Quality		
General Manager		[THE AUDITED ORGANIZATION]
Product Manager		[THE AUDITED ORGANIZATION]
Project Manager		[THE AUDITED ORGANIZATION]
Developing Prime		[THE AUDITED ORGANIZATION]
Dir. of Quality		[THE AUDITED ORGANIZATION]
Key Audit Contacts		[THE AUDITED ORGANIZATION]

1.2.2 The Results Report

This is the documented result of having (1) examined current documentation, (2) interviewed selected staff members, and (3) made other project observations. The Results Report will be objective, verifiable, and will contain no recommendations or other subjective expression of opinion. The results report is published by [the auditing organization] after review by the audited organization. Planned recipients, by responsibility are:

Responsibility	Name	Location
Product Manager		[THE AUDITED ORGANIZATION]
Project Manager		[THE AUDITED ORGANIZATION]
Developing Prime		[THE AUDITED ORGANIZATION]
Dir. of Quality		[THE AUDITED ORGANIZATION]
Key Audit Contacts		[THE AUDITED ORGANIZATION]

1.2.3 The Recommendations Report

This is the formal presentation of recommendations to [THE AUDITED ORGANIZATION] management. Recommendations are based on audit results, the business environment, and the past experiences and subjective judgements of the audit team. It is left to the recipients of this report to collaborate in decisions establishing priorities and to chart a course of action. Recommendations are published (and a response is requested) by [the auditing organization]. Planned recipients, by responsibility are:

Responsibility	Name	Location
Product Manager		[THE AUDITED ORGANIZATION]
Project Manager		[THE AUDITED ORGANIZATION]
Developing Prime		[THE AUDITED ORGANIZATION]
Dir. of Quality		[THE AUDITED ORGANIZATION]
Key Audit Contacts		[THE AUDITED ORGANIZATION]

1.2.4 The Executive Summary

Although there is a need to limit the ascent of unnecessary detail, a brief summary of audit activities, including an overview of recommendations, will be published by [the auditing organization]. Planned recipients, by responsibility are:

Responsibility	Name	Location
VP of Operations		
VP of Quality		
General Manager		[THE AUDITED ORGANIZATION]
Product Manager		[THE AUDITED ORGANIZATION]
Project Manager		[THE AUDITED ORGANIZATION]
Developing Prime		[THE AUDITED ORGANIZATION]
Dir. of Quality		[THE AUDITED ORGANIZATION]

2. PLAN REFINEMENT

2.1 Overview

This section of the plan will be used to document any plan changes.

2.2 History

The current issue of this plan is ISSUE 1, dated _____. No revisions are planned.

3. AUDIT ACTIVITIES

Four general methods of information gathering are used in characterizing the Software Quality Program: (1) Examination of process documentation, (2) Examination of selected in-process products, (3) Interview of staff, and (4) Process witnessing.

Key audit contacts (identified in Section 4) will be informed regularly of audit progress. Moreover, these contacts will regularly desk check the results report as it is being developed and will participate in a formal review of the final draft. Their participation in verifying report accuracy is critical to audit success.

3.1 Examination of Process Documentation

Quality Program Documentation will be examined for (1) coverage, (2) consistency and uniformity of purpose, and (3) adequacy. To reduce unwanted subjectivity and to find some meter for comparison, the *ANSI/IEEE Standard for Software Quality Assurance Plans* (ANSI/IEEE Std 730-1984) has been selected as representing reasonable and prudent coverage for documentation of this type.

The audit team will request specific documentation on initiating the audit. All documents considered in the program documentation analysis will be identified in the results report.

3.2 Examination of In-Process Products

Mr(s) _____ has been asked to provide sample in-process documentation representative of your work in the area. The audit team may request further examples or specific documents in their examination of Software Quality Program execution.

3.3 Staff Interviews

A small, but representative, sample of your staff from each of your teams will be interviewed, as will key liaisons in other organizations. These interviews will be performed away from the interviewees' offices, as coordinated by your key audit contacts, and will be of no more than 30 minutes in duration.

Materials will be provided to interviewees in advance so they can anticipate the questions to be asked. No more than two interviewers will be present and the atmosphere should be relaxed.

3.4 Process Witnessing

The Audit Team will be notified of all project-level meetings planned for the audit period. Also, the audit team will be afforded an opportunity to witness the following activities:

-
-
-

Their attendance at meetings, tours of facilities, and witnessing of specific project activities (for example, witnessing verification testing) is an important part of determining how the Software Quality Program is executed.

4. AUDIT TEAM PROFILE

Our team of xx professionals brings a total of over xx years of associated experience in the areas examined and is led by a seasoned chief auditor. Our interdisciplinary team has completed xx years/degrees of advanced study and is eager to assist your organization. The audit team is supplemented by key contacts from within your own organization (name them). These people, who know your organization and its successes, will assist in securing materials and facilities for the audit and will regularly review the results draft as it is being developed. They provide a critical role and we welcome them to our team.

APPENDIX to the PLAN: PLAN MILESTONES

_____Audit plan approval
_____Key organizational contacts identified and briefed
_____Documentation requested
_____Documentation delivered
_____Interviews scheduled
_____Interviews started
_____First results report draft issued to key contacts
_____Documentation analysis complete
_____Main interviews completed
_____Follow-up interviews complete
_____Characterization complete
_____Results report reviewed, revised, and published
_____Recommendations report published
_____Executive summary drafted
_____Executive summary reviewed, revised, and published
_____Response to recommendations received

RESULTS REPORT

Software Quality Program Audit of

[THE AUDITED ORGANIZATION]

1. INTRODUCTION

During [time period], [the auditing organization] performed a Software Quality Program Audit of [THE AUDITED ORGANIZATION, LOCATION]. The purpose of the audit was to ensure that [THE AUDITED ORGANIZATION] is subject to an effective Software Quality Program. The objective of the audit was two-fold:

- Determine how well the software quality program documentation addresses the basic elements of Software Quality Assurance.
- Determine how well the [THE AUDITED ORGANIZATION] follows its formal program.

This report presents no recommendations, but provides a quality process characterization to [THE AUDITED ORGANIZATION]. Statements in this results report are objective and verifiable; no subjective conclusions are drawn. Specific recommendations based on these documented results (and on various business factors) will be presented in a separate Audit Recommendations Report to be published [date].

2. AUDIT SCOPE

The scope of the audit covered [THE AUDITED ORGANIZATION, LOCATION] and its major external liaisons. This involved reviewing [name any key manual or document set] and other project documentation, as well as examining associated activities. There were, however, certain scope restrictions. Specifically, _____. The audit team worked very closely with [THE AUDITED ORGANIZATION] management and personnel to manage audit team interactions with the organization and to minimize interference with your current efforts.

3. AUDIT EXECUTION

Audit execution followed a formal plan [identifier] published on [date]. The content of that plan was:

- INTRODUCTION
- THE PLAN
    - 1- Introduction and Scope
        - 1.1- The Audit
        - 1.2- Report Distribution
    - 2- Plan Refinement (Overview and History)
    - 3- Process Characterization
        - 3.1- Examination of Process Documentation
        - 3.2- Examination of Selected In-process Products
        - 3.3- Interview of Staff
        - 3.4- Project Meeting Observations

4- Audit Process Status Reporting
   4.1- Regular Audit Results Reporting
   4.2- Final Reporting
5- Consultation
6- Audit Team Profile
7- PLAN MILESTONES

4. SOFTWARE QUALITY PROGRAM DOCUMENTATION ANALYSIS

This section of the results report presents the outcome of having examined applicable program documentation for (1) Coverage, (2) Consistency and uniformity of purpose, and (3) Adequacy. To reduce unwanted subjectivity and to find some meter for comparison, the *ANSI/IEEE Standard for Software Quality Assurance Plans* (ANSI/IEEE Std 730-1984) has been selected as representing reasonable and prudent coverage for documentation of this type. Department of Defense, NASA, or other industry standards could have been used.

The audit team requested specific documentation on initiating the audit. Analysis was limited, however, to documents readily available or received by the conclusion of the examination period. All documents considered in this analysis are listed in Appendix A. Those documents referenced by the xxx were considered part of that document for purposes of this evaluation. The audit team evaluated program documentation against the intent of the *ANSI/IEEE Standard* and its 13 elements: (1) Purpose, (2) Reference Documents,

(3) Management, (4) Documentation, (5) Standards, Practices, and Conventions, (6) Reviews and Audits, (7) Configuration Management, (8) Problem Reporting and Corrective Action (PRCA), (9) Tools, Techniques, and Methodologies, (10) Code Control, (11) Media Control, (12) Supplier Control, and (13) Records Collection, Maintenance, and Retention. The following subsections identify the extent to which each of the 13 elements above is covered by the documentation listed in Appendix A. Each starts with a quote from the *ANSI/IEEE Standard,* in italics, to summarize intended coverage for the element. Standard printing then resumes to present specific findings.

4.1 Purpose

"This section shall delineate the specific purpose and scope of the particular Software Quality Assurance Plan (SQAP). It shall list the name(s) of the software product items covered by the SQAP and the intended use of the software."

DIVERGENCE FROM *ANSI/IEEE STD 730-1984*:

DIVERGENCE FROM COMMON PRACTICE:

OTHER OBSERVATIONS:

4.2 Reference Documents

"This section shall provide a complete list of documents referenced elsewhere in the text of the plan."

DIVERGENCE FROM *ANSI/IEEE STD 730-1984*:

DIVERGENCE FROM COMMON PRACTICE:

OTHER OBSERVATIONS:

4.3 Management

"This section shall describe the organization, tasks, and responsibilities."

DIVERGENCE FROM *ANSI/IEEE STD 730-1984*:

DIVERGENCE FROM COMMON PRACTICE:

OTHER OBSERVATIONS:

4.4 Documentation

"This section shall: 1) Identify the documentation governing the development, verification and validation, use, and maintenance of the software, and 2) State how the documents are to be used for adequacy. The statement shall include identification of the review or audit by which the adequacy of each document shall be confirmed, with reference to the Plan."

DIVERGENCE FROM *ANSI/IEEE STD 730-1984*:

DIVERGENCE FROM COMMON PRACTICE:

OTHER OBSERVATIONS:

4.5 Standards, Practices, and Conventions

"This section shall: 1) Identify the standards, practices, and conventions to be applied, and 2) State how compliance with these items is to be monitored and assured."

DIVERGENCE FROM *ANSI/IEEE STD 730-1984*:

DIVERGENCE FROM COMMON PRACTICE:

OTHER OBSERVATIONS:

4.6 Reviews and Audits

"This section shall: 1) Define the technical and managerial reviews and audits to be conducted, and 2) State how the reviews and audits are to be accomplished."

DIVERGENCE FROM *ANSI/IEEE STD 730-1984*:

DIVERGENCE FROM COMMON PRACTICE:

OTHER OBSERVATIONS:

4.7 Configuration Management

"This section shall document the methods to be used for identifying the software product items, controlling and implementing changes, and recording and reporting change implementation status. This documentation shall either be provided explicitly in this section or by reference to an existing software configuration management plan."

DIVERGENCE FROM *ANSI/IEEE STD 730-1984*:

DIVERGENCE FROM COMMON PRACTICE:

OTHER OBSERVATIONS:

4.8 Problem Reporting and Corrective Action (PRCA)

"This section shall: 1) Describe the practices and procedures to be followed for reporting, tracking, and resolving software problems, and 2) State the specific organizational responsibilities concerned with their implementation."

DIVERGENCE FROM *ANSI/IEEE STD 730-1984*:

DIVERGENCE FROM COMMON PRACTICE:

OTHER OBSERVATIONS:

4.9 Tools, Techniques, and Methodologies

"This section shall identify the special software tools, techniques, and methodologies employed on the specific project that support Quality Assurance, state their purposes, and describe their use."

DIVERGENCE FROM *ANSI/IEEE STD 730-1984*:

DIVERGENCE FROM COMMON PRACTICE:

OTHER OBSERVATIONS:

4.10 Code Control

"This section shall define the methods and facilities used to maintain and store controlled versions of identified software. This may be implemented in conjunction with a Computer Program Library."

DIVERGENCE FROM *ANSI/IEEE STD 730-1984*:

DIVERGENCE FROM COMMON PRACTICE:

OTHER OBSERVATIONS:

4.11 Media Control

"This section shall state the methods and facilities to be used to protect computer program physical media from unauthorized access or inadvertent damage or degradation."

DIVERGENCE FROM *ANSI/IEEE STD 730-1984*:

DIVERGENCE FROM COMMON PRACTICE:

OTHER OBSERVATIONS:

4.12 Supplier Control

This section shall state the provisions for assuring that vendor-provided and subcontractor-developed software meets established technical requirements. As a minimum the supplier shall be required to prepare and implement a Software Quality Assurance Plan in accordance with this standard.

DIVERGENCE FROM *ANSI/IEEE STD 730-1984*:

DIVERGENCE FROM COMMON PRACTICE:

OTHER OBSERVATIONS:

4.13 Records Collection, Maintenance, and Retention

"This section shall identify the SQA documentation to be retained; shall state the methods and facilities to be used to assemble, safeguard, and maintain this documentation; and shall designate the retention period."

DIVERGENCE FROM *ANSI/IEEE STD 730-1984*:

DIVERGENCE FROM COMMON PRACTICE:

OTHER OBSERVATIONS:

5. ANALYSIS OF QUALITY PROGRAM EXECUTION

5.1 PROCESS MODEL

Audit findings pertinent to specific phases, as identified in project documentation, are presented using the following format:

- Definition: A discussion of how specific activities are defined for the project phase.
- Deliverables: A discussion of outputs provided by the phase.
- Verification and Validation: A discussion of those V&V activities defined to "check" products built in the phase.
- Liaisons: A discussion of critical interfaces.

5.1.1 Phase 1: [Phase Name]

5.1.1.1 Definition

5.1.1.2 Deliverables

5.1.1.3 Verification and Validation

5.1.1.4 Liaisons

5.1.N ..... Phase N: [Phase Name]

Continue for each phase

5.2 Process Controls

Local control elements discussed in this section include project management, configuration management, and quality management.

5.2.1 Project Management

5.2.2 Configuration Management

5.2.3 Quality Management

5.3 PROCESS ENVIRONMENT

Environmental issues, although outside the direct control of local management, play an important role in project success or failure. In discussing key environmental issues addressed by the audit, this section comprises: The Organizational Structure; Major External Interfaces; The Tools, Workbenches, and Environments; Available Training; and The Local Quality Culture.

5.3.1 Organizational Structure

Although it has never been the intent of the *ANSI/IEEE Std 730-1984* to promote a specific structure, organizational structure is an important environmental factor. It can obstruct, as well as ease, communication and control.

5.3.2 External Interfaces

5.3.3 Tools, Workbenches, and Environments

5.3.4 Training

5.3.5 Culture

6. AUDIT SUMMARY

The goal of this Software Quality Process Audit was to determine whether a reasonable and prudent methodology was well documented and applied to [THE AUDITED ORGANIZATION, LOCATION]. That issue is of vital importance because the process of software development must be understood and controlled before positive process evolution is possible. Standards, the backbone of control, cost money. They must be developed, disseminated, maintained, and their application confirmed. Results must be analyzed to ensure the effectiveness of applicable standards. Because "more" is not better when it comes standards, both scope and depth are important issues in standards design. This audit shows xxxxx in these areas. People working in xxx organizations showed a strong desire to produce a quality product. This is evident from the cooperation the audit team received in obtaining interviews and from the open and frank discussions held. Both management and staff recognized the need for a flexible yet disciplined methodology for their development process.

Most of the process problems center on these themes:

-
-

Most quality program documentation problems centered on these different, though related, themes:

-
-

Please refer back to the body of the report for specific details.

SIGNATURE BLOCK

RECOMMENDATIONS REPORT

Software Quality Program Audit of

[THE AUDITED ORGANIZATION]

1. INTRODUCTION

During [time frame], [the auditing organization] performed a Software Quality Program Audit of [THE AUDITED ORGANIZATION]. The purpose of the audit was to ensure that xxxx is subject to an effective Software Quality Program.

An Audit Results Report was published on [date] to document:

- How the software quality program documentation addresses the basic elements of Software Quality Assurance.
- How the xxxx organization follows its formal program.

Please refer to the Audit Results Report for detailed findings. Audit execution followed an Audit Plan published on [date].

The purpose of this Audit Recommendations Report is to present specific recommendations based on the Audit Results Report. These recommendations have been tempered by various business attributes of the [THE AUDITED ORGANIZATION].

Each recommendation presented herein will consist of:

- Concise statement of recommendation
- Summary of supporting evidence
- Perceived implementation costs and expected benefits
- Risk of no action

For the reader's convenience, all recommendations are restated without their supporting discussions in a special "Summary" section of this report.

Please note that process improvements do not always require increased expenditures and effort. Excessive control and perfectionism are to be avoided as much as inadequate control and unpredictable quality.

2. BUSINESS ENVIRONMENT

The audit team's objective is to evaluate the particular methodologies used by [THE AUDITED ORGANIZATION] and determine their effectiveness based on the needs of the organization. Several project-dependent factors are assessed to determine which quality issues are most critical to [THE AUDITED ORGANIZATION] and to determine needs. These factors include project size, newness, nature of the application, criticality to marketing, staff experience, customer expectations, quality reputation, product life cycle, and future expectations. Specific areas of interest include:

-
-

3. RECOMMENDATIONS

Recommendations presented in this report are categorized and presented by the process perspective to which they apply. Specifically, they are:

- Model-Related Recommendations
- Control-Related Recommendations
- Environmental Recommendations

It is left to the recipients of this report to collaborate in decisions establishing priorities and to chart a course of action.

3.1 Model-Related Recommendations

Recommendations that relate directly to the process model are most easily implemented by those groups and individuals closest to the specific process involved. For this reason, these recommendations can often be the quickest to implement within a limited budget and can provide immediate return on improvement efforts. The emphasis here is on doing things right.

[M1] [One-line statement] (repeat this template for each recommendation)

SUPPORT:

IMPACT:

RISK OF NO ACTION:

3.2 Control-Related Recommendations

As contrasted with model-related recommendations that can help us do things right, control-related recommendations can help us to do the right things. Specifically, control allows the removal of roadblocks, consistency of process application, and the consolidation (and retention) of gains. Recommendations in this category tend to require a greater consistency of purpose, coordination at higher levels, and management commitment. Therefore, activities in response to these recommendations invest in our future rather than giving us immediate return on investment.

[C1] [One-line statement] (repeat this template for each recommendation)

SUPPORT:

IMPACT:

RISK OF NO ACTION:

3.3 Environmental Recommendations

As seen in the preceding section, definition and flow of control is crucial. So, however, is the consistency and flow of data (that is, communications paths, informal networks, information sources, and so on). Recommendations that relate to the development process environment address information, the local culture, the existence or use of tools, and similar issues. Recommendations in this category can have a wide range of involvement with some only requiring local group consensus and others the support of upper management.

[E1] [One-line statement] (repeat this template for each recommendation.)

SUPPORT:

IMPACT:

RISK OF NO ACTION:

4. SUMMARY

For the reader's convenience, recommendations are restated here without the supporting details provided in the body of this report. These recommendations cover the Process Model (PM.n), Process Controls (PC.n), and the Process Environment (PE.n).

[M.1]

-
-
-

[C.1]

-
-
-

[E.1]

-
-
-

5. CONCLUSION

We hope that with these recommendations from an external observer, we have provided a service that will assist you in continuing the evolution of your already commendable program.

To assist in meeting this objective, [the auditing organization] extends an offer of consultation. A formal written response is requested to inform us, in general terms, about those process changes you (as an organization) intend to implement as a result of these recommendations. The response should also respond to our offer of consultation. We thank you in advance for your cooperation.

Please do not hesitate to call [contact and number] with any comments or questions.

[SIGNATURE BLOCK]

EXECUTIVE SUMMARY

Software Quality Program Audit of

[THE AUDITED ORGANIZATION]

1. INTRODUCTION

During [time frame], [the auditing organization] performed a Software Quality Program Audit of [THE AUDITED ORGANIZATION]. The purpose of the audit was to ensure that xxxx is subject to an effective Software Quality Program.

An Audit Results Report was published on [date] to document:

- How the software quality program documentation addresses the basic elements of Software Quality Assurance.
- How the [THE AUDITED ORGANIZATION] organization follows its formal program.

The purpose of this Executive Summary is to provide an overview of findings and recommendations tempered by various business attributes of the [THE AUDITED ORGANIZATION].

2. BUSINESS ENVIRONMENT

The audit team's objective is to evaluate the particular methodologies used by [THE AUDITED ORGANIZATION] and determine their effectiveness based on the needs of the organization. Several project-dependent factors are assessed to determine which quality issues are most critical to [THE AUDITED ORGANIZATION] and to determine needs. These factors include project size, newness, nature of the application, criticality to marketing, staff experience, customer expectations, quality reputation, product life cycle, and future expectations. Specific areas of interest include:

-
-

3. RESULTS

The goal of this Software Quality Process Audit was to determine whether a reasonable and prudent methodology was well-documented and applied to [THE AUDITED ORGANIZATION, LOCATION]. That issue is of vital importance because the process of software development must be understood and controlled before positive process evolution is possible. Standards, the backbone of control, cost money. They must be developed, disseminated, maintained, and their application confirmed. Results must be analyzed to ensure the effectiveness of applicable standards. Because "more" is not better when it comes standards, both scope and depth are important issues in standards design. This audit shows xxxxx in these areas. People working in xxx organizations showed a strong desire to produce a quality product. This is evident from the cooperation the audit team received in obtaining interviews and from the open and frank discussions held. Both management and staff recognized the need for a flexible yet disciplined methodology for their development process.

Most of the process problems center on these themes:

-
-

Most quality program documentation problems centered on these different, though related, themes:

-
-

4. RECOMMENDATIONS

Recommendations presented to your organization were categorized and presented by the process perspective to which they apply. Specifically, these perspectives are:

- Model-Related Recommendations. Recommendations that relate directly to the process model are most easily implemented by those groups and individuals closest to the specific process involved. For this reason, these recommendations can often be the quickest to implement within a limited budget and can provide immediate return on improvement efforts. The emphasis here is on doing things right.

- Control-Related Recommendations. As contrasted with model-related recommendations that can help you do things right, control-related recommendations can help you do the right things. Specifically, control allows the removal of roadblocks, consistency of process

application, and the consolidation (and retention) of gains. Recommendations in this category tend to require a greater consistency of purpose, coordination at higher levels, and management commitment. Therefore, activities in response to these recommendations invest in our future rather than giving us immediate return on investment.
- Environmental Recommendations. As seen in the preceding section, definition and flow of control is crucial. So, however, is the consistency and flow of data (that is, communications paths, informal networks, information sources, et cetera). Recommendations that relate to the development process environment address information, the local culture, the existence or use of tools, and similar issues. Recommendations in this category can have a wide range of involvement with some only requiring local group consensus and others the support of upper management.

For your convenience, recommendations from the original report are restated here without the supporting details provided in the body of this report. These recommendations cover the Process Model (PM.n), Process Controls (PC.n), and the Process Environment (PE.n).

[M.1]

-
-

[C.1]

-
-

[E.1]

-
-

5. CONCLUSION

We hope that with these recommendations from an external observer, we have provided a service that will assist you in continuing the evolution of your already commendable program. It is left to the recipients of this report to collaborate in decisions establishing priorities and to chart a course of action.

To assist in meeting this objective, [the auditing organization] extends an offer of consultation. A formal written response is requested to inform us, in general terms, about those process changes you (as an organization) intend to implement as a result of these recommendations. The response should also respond to our offer of consultation. We thank you in advance for your cooperation.

Please do not hesitate to call [contact and number] with any comments or questions.

[SIGNATURE BLOCK]

TEST VERIFICATION REPORT
(TVR)

The Test Effort

TYPE: _____   **TROUBLE #:** _____
        Select from Below   If Applicable

[1] Integration Test Verification Report

[2] Feature (or Subsystem) Test Verification Report

[3] System Test Verification Report

[4] Product Test in support of Audit: _____
                                                     specify

[5] Other: _____
              specify

RELEASE: _____   **LOAD:** _____

WORK PRODUCT ID: _____

TEST PLAN IDENTIFIER(s): _____

The People

DEVELOPMENT ENGINEERS:

Release Engineer: _____

Dept/Loc: _____   Ext: _____

Subsystem Engineer: _____

Dept/Loc: _____   Ext: _____

Feature Engineer: _____

Dept/Loc: _____   Ext: _____

TEST ENGINEERS:

Test Plan Engineer: _____

Dept/Loc: _____   Ext: _____

Test Coordinator: _____

Dept/Loc: _____   Ext: _____

The Report

Prepared by: _____   **Approved by:** _____

Printed Name: _____   Printed Name: _____

Date: _____   Date: _____

PROCEDURE EVALUATION —

Total Product Size: _____ % code coverage: _____

Tests Identified: _____   Tests Executed: _____

Tests Successful: _____

As needed, use the space below and any additional sheets or attachments to provide any further discussion of test procedures.

RESOURCES USE —

Total # testers involved: _____ Average experience: _____ yrs.

Experience ranges From: _____ To: _____ years.

Scheduled Lab Time: _____ hours.

Unscheduled Lab Down Time: _____ hours.

(Total # Defects Found) ÷ (Sched. Lab Time − Lab Down Time) = _____ def/hr.

Provide any additional discussion of using the laboratory or staff. Highlight availability and usefulness. Use additional sheets or attachments as needed.

TOOL USE: Wherever test tool difficulties occur, use additional sheets or attachments as necessary to:

Identify *tool* and its configuration or issue:
_____
_____
_____
_____
_____

Describe the *extent of tool use* as a percent of its functionality:
_____
_____
_____
_____
_____

Describe the *extent of tool use* as a percent of its functionality:
_____% and the *duration of its use* relative to total test time:_____%
Identify and discuss the problem/deficiency and its effect on the test effort.
_____
_____
_____
_____
_____
_____
_____

DEFECT SUMMARY—

Total Trouble Reports written during this test effort against
this product: _____   other products: _____

Total *UNRESOLVED* Trouble Reports written during this test effort against
this product: _____   other products: _____

ID #s for UNRESOLVED trouble reports against

this product: other products:

_____   _____   _____   _____
_____   _____   _____   _____
_____   _____   _____   _____
_____   _____   _____   _____
_____   _____   _____   _____
_____   _____   _____   _____
_____   _____   _____   _____
_____   _____   _____   _____
_____   _____   _____   _____
_____   _____   _____   _____
_____   _____   _____   _____
_____   _____   _____   _____

OTHER OPEN ITEMS—

Describe any other pertinent open items below or on a separate attachment, following the format provided.

Identify and Describe:

Discuss the *effect* of this open item and its resolution on this (and other) releases.
_____
_____
_____

Identify the *Action Plan* owner (organization, group, or individual). If the specific action plan is known, briefly describe it.
_____
_____
_____

REFERENCES—
_____
_____
_____

SIGBLOCK

INSPECTION PLANS AND REPORTS

Weekly Inspection Report

Page 1

INSPECTIONS OPEN MORE THAN 14 DAYS AS OF __/__/__
mo/da/yr

Release Stream	Tracking Identifier	Work Brkdn Structure ID	DESCRIPTION	Inspection Information			
				Date	Type	DISP	Forms OK?

WEEKLY DEFECT SUMMARY BLOCK

	CO	DA	HW	FW	IF	LO	PE	SC	WF	WG	AM	OT	Totals
M	/	/	/	/	/	/	/	/	/	/	/	/	/
W	/	/	/	/	/	/	/	/	/	/	/	/	/
E	/	/	/	/	/	/	/	/	/	/	/	/	/
Totals	/	/	/	/	/	/	/	/	/	/	/	/	/
P	/	/	/	/	/	/	/	/	/	/	/	/	/
Totals	/	/	/	/	/	/	/	/	/	/	/	/	/

WEEKLY INSPECTION COST SUMMARY BLOCK

TOTAL PREP TIME (Ave prep time × number of attendees) =	
ADJUSTED INSPECTION TIME (Inspection time × number of attendees) =	
VERIFICATION TIME (Total prep time + Adjusted inspection time) =	
INSPECTION COST (Verification time × staff multiplier) =	
REWORK TIME:	
REWORK COST (Rework time × staff multiplier)	

Pages 2 to n

INDIVIDUAL INSPECTION SUMMARY

IDENTIFICATION BLOCK

Release Stream	Tracking Identifier	Work Brkdn Structure ID	DESCRIPTION	Inspection Information			
				Date	Type	DISP	Forms OK?

INSPECTION NUMBER: Audit ID: CLOSE DATE:
(initial, first reinspection, etc) (if applicable)

DEFECT SUMMARY BLOCK

	CO	DA	HW	FW	IF	LO	PE	SC	WF	WG	AM	OT	Totals
M	/	/	/	/	/	/	/	/	/	/	/	/	/
W	/	/	/	/	/	/	/	/	/	/	/	/	/
E	/	/	/	/	/	/	/	/	/	/	/	/	/
Totals	/	/	/	/	/	/	/	/	/	/	/	/	/
P	/	/	/	/	/	/	/	/	/	/	/	/	/
Totals	/	/	/	/	/	/	/	/	/	/	/	/	/

MULTIPLIER BLOCK
STAFF HOUR COST: _____ = STAFF MULTIPLIER

INSPECTION COST SUMMARY BLOCK

TOTAL PREP TIME (Ave prep time × number of attendees) =	
ADJUSTED INSPECTION TIME (Inspection time × number of attendees) =	
VERIFICATION TIME (Total prep time + Adjusted inspection time) =	
INSPECTION COST (Verification time × staff multiplier) =	
REWORK TIME:	
REWORK COST (Rework time × staff multiplier)	

MONTHLY INSPECTION SUMMARY

Page 1

| INSPECTIONS HELD BETWEEN __/__/__ AND __/__/__ |
| mo/da/yr   mo/da/yr |

Release Stream	Tracking Identifier	Work Brkdn Structure ID	DESCRIPTION	Inspection Information			
				Date	Type	DISP	Forms OK?

Page 2 to n

Prerelease Inspection Summaries
(By WBS Structure for the _____ RLSE Stream)

Work Breakdn	# Insp	# Defects Severity		Cost		/kloc	/insp	/hr	DEFECTS Percent				DISP		
		1	2	Insp	Rewrk				WF	WG	AM	OT	1	2	3

APPENDIX 5

References

References provided here are a mix of offerings designed to support the text and to start your reviews and audits library. Some of the references, you will note, are somewhat old. When I was working on my master's degree at Northwestern under Professor Albert Rubenstein, it bothered me a great deal that many of the references he provided were seemingly out of date. It took a while, discovering what was already discovered, before the realization came that once a concept is established as true or pertinent, it remains so until shown otherwise. Therefore you will find some of the earlier offerings in the literature for topics covered in the text. Besides, who would not want a copy of Fagan's original papers on inspections? I hope the references will be useful to you.

IEEE STANDARDS

Copies of approved ANSI/IEEE Standards may be obtained from The IEEE Service Center, 201 Hoes Lane, Piscataway, N.J. 08854.

[IEEE, 729]: ANSI/IEEE Std 729-1983, *IEEE Standard Glossary of Software Engineering Terminology.*

[IEEE, 730]: ANSI/IEEE Std 730-1984, *IEEE Standard for Software Quality Assurance Plans.*

[IEEE, 1012]: ANSI/IEEE Std 1012-1986, *IEEE Standard for Software Verification and Validation Plans.*

[IEEE, 1028]: ANSI/IEEE Std 1028-1988, *IEEE Standard for Software Reviews and Audits.*

DEPARTMENT OF DEFENSE STANDARDS

Copies of these standards may be obtained from the Commanding Officer, Naval Publications and Forms Center, 5801 Tabor Avenue, Philadelphia, PA 19120.

[DOD, 1521B]: MIL-STD-1521B, June 1985, *Technical Reviews and Audits for Systems, Equipments, and Computer Software*.

[DOD, 2167]: DOD-STD-2167, June 1985, *Defense Systems Software Development*.

[DOD, 2167A]: DOD-STD-2167A, February 28, 1988, *Defense Systems Software Development*.

[DOD, 2168]: DOD-STD-2168, DRAFT, *Defense Systems Software Quality Program*.

BOOKS

[BOEHM, 1981] Barry W. Boehm, *Software Engineering Economics*, Englewood Cliffs, NJ: Prentice Hall.

[BRYAN, 1988] William L. Bryan and Stanley G. Siegel, *Software Product Assurance—Techniques for Reducing Software Risk*, New York: Elsevier.

[CLELAND, 1975] David I. Cleland and William R. King, *Systems Analysis and Project Management*, New York: McGraw-Hill.

[CLELAND, 1983] D. I. Cleland and W. R. King (Eds.), *Project Management Handbook*, New York: Van Nostrand Reinhold, Inc.

[CONTE, 1986] S. D. Conte, H. E. Dunsmore, and V. Y. Shen, *Software Engineering Metrics and Models*, Menlo Park, CA: Benjamin/Cummings.

[COOPER, 1979] John D. Cooper and Matthew J. Fisher (Eds.), *Software Quality Management*, New York: Petrocelli Books, Inc.

[DeMARCO, 1982] T. DeMarco, *Controlling Software Project Management Measurement and Estimation*, New York: Yourdon Press.

[DEUTSCH, 1982] M. S. Deutsch, *Software Verification and Validation*, Englewood Cliffs, NJ: Prentice Hall.

[EVANS, 1983] M. Evans, P. Piazza, and J. Dolkas, *Principles of Productive Software Management*, New York: Wiley-Interscience.

[FREEDMAN, 1982] D. P. Freedman and G. M. Wienberg, *Handbook of Walkthroughs, Inspections, and Technical Reviews*, Boston: Little, Brown.

[HUMPHREY, 1989] W. S. Humphrey, *Managing the Software Process*, Reading, MA: Addison-Wesley.

[JURAN, 1964] J. Juran, *Managerial Breakthrough*, New York: McGraw-Hill.

[JURAN, 1974] J. M. Juran, F. M. Gryna, and R. S. Bingham, *Quality Control Handbook*, Third Edition, New York: McGraw-Hill.

[JURAN, 1980] J. Juran, *Quality Planning and Analysis*, New York: McGraw-Hill.

[METZGER, 1981] P. W. Metzger, *Managing a Programming Project*, Englewood Cliffs, NJ: Prentice Hall.

[SCHULMEYER, 1987] G. G. Schulmeyer and J. I. McManus (Eds.), *Handbook of Software Quality Assurance*, New York: Van Nostrand Reinhold.

[TAUSWORTHE, 1979] R. C. Tausworthe, *Standardized Development of Computer Software*, Englewood Cliffs, NJ: Prentice Hall.

[TURNER, 1980] W. Stephen Turner, *Project Auditing Methodology*, New York: North-Holland.

[YOURDON, 1978] E. Yourdon, *Structured Walkthroughs*, New York: Yourdon.

ARTICLES

[Adrion, 1982] W. R. Adrion, M. A. Branstad, and J. C. Cherniavsky, "Validation, Verification, and Testing of Computer Software," *ACM Computing Surveys*, Vol. 14, No. 2, pp. 159–192.

[Azuma, 1981] M. Azuma and T. Mizuno, "Steps Integrated Software Standards and Its Productivity Impact," *Proceedings of IEEE Compcon September, 1981*, pp. 83–95.

[Balzer, 1983] R. Balzer, T. E. Cheatham, and C. Green, "Software Technology in the 1990's: Using a New Paradigm," *Computer*, Vol. 16, No. 8, pp. 39–45.

[Beck, 1983] L. L. Beck and T. E. Perkins, "A Survey of Software Engineering Practice: Tools, Methods, and Results," *IEEE Transactions on Software Engineering*, Vol. 9, No. 5, pp. 541–561.

[Bergland, 1981] G. D. Bergland, "A Guided Tour of Program Design Methodologies," *Computer*, Vol. 14, No. 10, pp. 13–37.

[Bersoff, 1979] E. H. Bersoff, et al., "Software Configuration Management A Tutorial," *Computer*, Vol. 12, No. 1, pp. 6–14.

[Bersoff, 1984] E. H. Bersoff, "Elements of Software Configuration Management," *IEEE Transactions on Software Engineering*, Vol. 10, No. 1, pp. 79–87.

[Boehm, 1975] B. W. Boehm, "The High Cost of Software," *IEEE TUTORIAL Software Testing and Validation Techniques*, 2nd Edition, pp. 444–455.

[Boehm, 1984.a] B. W. Boehm, "Software Engineering Economics," *Transactions on Software Engineering*, Vol. 10, No. 1, pp. 4–21.

[Boehm, 1984.b] B. W. Boehm, "Verifying and Validating Software Requirements and Design Specifications," *Software*, Vol. 1, No. 1, pp. 75–88.

[Boehm, 1984.c] B. W. Boehm, T. E. Gray, and T. Seewaldt, "Prototyping vs. Specifying A Multi-Project Experiment," *Proceedings of the 7th Int.Conf. on Software Engineering March 26-29, 1984*, pp. 473–485.

[Boehm, 1984.d] B. Boehm, M. Penedo, E. D. Stuckle, R. D. Williams, and A. B. Pyster, "A Software Development Environment for Improving Productivity," *Computer*, Vol. 17, No. 6, pp. 30–34.

[Boehm, 1987] B. Boehm, "Improving Software Productivity," *Computer*, Vol. 20, No. 9, pp. 43–58.

[Boehm, 1988] Barry Boehm, "A Spiral Model of Software Development and Enhancement," *Computer*, Vol. 21, No. 5, pp. 61–72.

[Bryan, 1982] W. L. Bryan, et al., "Auditing Throughout The Software Life Cycle," *Computer*, Vol. 15, No. 3, pp. 57–67.

[Cox, 1988] J. L. Cox and P. B. Dinsdale, "Selling New Ideas Properly Aids Their Acceptance Within an Organization," *IEEE Engineering Management Review*, Vol. 16, No.1, pp. 38–44.

[Craven, 1986] L. A. Craven, H. Oehring, J. B. Sharpless, and L. C. Stecher, "Engineering the 5ESS Switch Architecture A Design to Support the Evolving ISDN Standards and

Technology," *Sixth International Conference on Software Engineering for Telecommunication Switching Systems*, Systems Conf. Publ. No. 259, pp. 124–127.

[Curtis, 1984] B. Curtis, "Fifteen Years of Psychology in Software Engineering Individual Differences and Cognitive Science," *Proceedings of the 7th International Conference on Software Engineering March 26-29, 1984*, pp. 97–107.

[Deutsch, 1981] M. S. Deutsch, "Software Project Verification and Validation," *Computer*, Vol. 14, No. 4, pp. 54–69.

[Fagan, 1976] M. E. Fagan, "Design and Code Inspections to Reduce Errors in Program Development," *IBM Systems Journal*, Vol. 15 No. 3, pp. 182–211.

[Fagan, 1977] M. E. Fagan, "Inspecting Software Design and Code." *Datamation*, Vol. 23, No. 10, pp. 133–144.

[Forman, 1981] J. J. Forman, "How Much Does Configuration Management Cost?" *Proceedings of the Software Engineering Standards Application Workshop, August, 1981*, pp. 41–44.

[Fujii, 1977] M. S. Fujii, "Independent Verification of Highly Reliable Programs," *Proceedings of the Computer Software and Applications Conference, November, 1977*, pp. 38–44.

[Fujii, 1978] M. S. Fujii, "A Comparison of Software Assurance Methods," *Proceedings of the Software Quality and Assurance Workshop, November, 1978*, pp. 27–32.

[Glass, 1981.a] R. L. Glass, "Persistent Software Errors," *IEEE Transactions on Software Engineering*, Vol. 7, No. 2, pp. 162–168.

[Glass, 1981.b] R. L. Glass, "Standards for Standards Writers," *Proceedings of The Software Engineering Standards Applications Workshop, August, 1981*, pp. 144–146.

[Golonski, 1987] William Golonski, "New Product Planning Organizational Issues for Success," *Quality Progress*, Vol. 20, No. 6, pp. 16–17.

[Goodenough, 1980] J. B. Goodenough and C. L. McGowan, "Software Quality Assurance Testing and Validation," *Proceedings of the IEEE*, Vol. 68, No. 9, pp. 1093–1098.

[Greene, 1982] J. J. Greene, C. P. Hollocker, M. A. Jones, and T. C. Pingel, "Developing A Software Quality Assurance Program Based On The IEEE Standard 730-1981," *Proceedings of the IEEE Computer Software and Applications Conference, November, 1982*, pp. 257–262.

[Gustafson, 1982] G. G. Gustafson, and R. J. Kerr, "Some Practical Experiences with a Software Quality Assurance Program," *Communications of the ACM*, Vol. 25, No. 1, pp. 4–12.

[Hansen, 1983] J. V. Hansen, "Audit Considerations in Distributed Processing Systems," *Communications of the ACM*, vol. 26, No. 8, pp. 562–569.

[Hoare, 1987] C. A. R. Hoare, "An Overview of Some Formal Methods for Program Design," *Computer* Vol. 20, No. 9, pp. 85–91.

[Hollocker, 1986] Charles P. Hollocker, "Finding the Cost of Software Quality," *IEEE Transactions on Engineering Management*, Vol. EM-33, No. 4, pp. 223–228.

[Hora, 1988] M. E. Hora, "The Unglamorous Game of Managing Maintenance," *IEEE Engineering Management Review*, Vol. 16, No. 1, pp. 12–21.

[Howden, 1981] W. E. Howden, "Life-Cycle Software Validation," *Computer* Vol. 15, No. 2, pp. 326–333.

[Howes, 1984] Norman Howes, "Managing Software Development Projects for Maximum Productivity," *IEEE Transactions on Software Engineering*, Vol. SE-10, No. 1, pp. 27–35.

[Humphrey, 1988] Watts Humphrey, "Characterizing the Software Process," *IEEE Software*, Vol. 5, No. 3, pp. 73–79.

[Ingrassia, 1976] F. S. Ingrassia, "The Unit Development Folder (UDF): An Effective Management Tool For Software Development," *TRW Technical Report TRW-SS-76-11*, October, 1976.

[Kenny, 1988] Andrew Kenny, "A New Paradigm for Quality Assurance" *Quality Progress*, Vol. XXI, No. 6, pp. 30–34.

[Litecky, 1981] C. R. Litecky and L. E. Rittenburg, "The External Auditor's Review of Computer Controls," *Communications of the ACM*, Vol. 24, No. 5, pp. 288–295.

[Mandt, 1983] Edward J. Mandt, "A Basic Model of Manager Development," *IEEE Transactions on Engineering Management*, Vol. EM-30, No. 4, pp. 54–57.

[McGowan, 1985] C. McGowan, M. Feblowitz, and M. Chandarsekharan, "The METAFOR Approach to Executable Specifications," *IEEE Proceedings of the 3rd Int. Workshop on Software Specification & Design August, 1985*, pp. 163–169.

[McKee, 1986] John B. McKee, "Computer User Manuals in Print: Do They Have a Future," *Asterisk*, Vol. 12, No. 2, pp. 11–19.

[Methodios, 1976] I. Methodios, "Internal Controls and Audit," *Journal of System Management*, Vol. 27, No. 6, pp. 6–14.

[Mills, 1988] H. D. Mills, "Stepwise Refinement and Verification in Box-Structured Systems" *Computer*, Vol. 21, No. 6, pp. 23–36.

[Munro, 1988] H. Munro and H. Noori, "Measuring Commitment to New Manufacturing Technology: Integrating Technological Push and Marketing Pull Concepts," *IEEE Transactions on Engineering Management*, Vol. 35, No. 2, pp. 63–70.

[Musa, 1985] J. D. Musa, "Software Engineering: The Future of a Profession," *Software*, Vol. 2, No. 1, pp. 55–62.

[Myers, 1978]: G. J. Myers, "A Controlled Experiment in Program Testing and Code Walk-throughs/Inspections," *Communications of the ACM*, Vol. 21, No. 9, pp. 760–768.

[Parnas, 1985] D. L. Parnas and D. M. Weiss, "Active Design Reviews: Principles and Practices," *NRL Report 8927*, Computer Science and Systems Branch, Information Technology Division, November 18, 1985, pp. 1–10.

[Parnas, 1987] D. L. Parnas and D. M. Weiss, "Active Design Reviews: Principles and Practices," *The Journal of Systems and Software*, Vol. 7, No. 3, Sept., pp. 259–265.

[Poensgen, 1983] Otto Poensgen and Helmut Hort, "R&D Management and Financial Performance," *IEEE Transactions on Engineering Management*, Vol. EM-30, No. 4, pp. 212–221.

[Prell, 1984] E. M. Prell and A. P. Sheng, "Building Quality and Productivity into a Large Software System," *IEEE Software*, Vol. 1, No. 7, pp. 46–54.

[Royce, 1970] W. W. Royce, "Managing the Development of Large Software Systems: Concepts and Techniques," Proceedings, WESCON, August, 1970.

[Schmidt, 1988] M. J. Schmidt, "Schedule Monitoring of Engineering Projects," *IEEE Transactions on Engineering Management*, Vol. 35, No. 2, pp. 108–113.

[Schneiderman, 1988] Arthur Schneiderman, "Setting Quality Goals," *Quality Progress*, Vol. 21, No. 4, pp. 51–57.

[Schroeder, 1984] A. Schroeder, "Integrated Program Measurement and Documentation Tools," *Proceedings of the 7th International Conference on Software Engineering*, March, 1984, pp. 304–313.

[Sullivan, 1988] Lawrence Sullivan, "Policy Management Through Quality Function Deployment," *Quality Progress*, Vol. XXI, No. 6, pp. 18–22.

[Tai, 1985] K. C. Tai and C. Y. Din, "Validation of Concurrency in Software Specification and Design," *IEEE Proceedings of the 3rd Int. Workshop on Software Specification & Design*, August, 1985, pp. 223–227.

[Thayer, 1981] R. Thayer, A. Pyster, and R. Wood, "Major Issues in Software Engineering Project Management," *IEEE Transactions on Software Engineering*, Vol. SE-7, No.4, pp. 333–342.

[Weinberg, 1984] G. M. Weinberg and D. P. Freedman, "Reviews, Walkthroughs, and Inspections in Project Management Systems," *IEEE Transactions on Software Engineering*, Vol. 10, No. 1, pp. 49–59.

[Weiss, 1979] David M. Weiss, "Evaluating Software Development by Error Analysis: The Data from the Architecture Research Facility," *The Journal of Systems and Software*, Vol. 1, No. 1, pp. 57–70.

INDEX

Acceptance criteria, 37
Audit, 65
   activities, 68, 70, 71, 73, 74
   authority, 18, 19, 22
   commitment, 76
   communication and judgment barriers, 76
   definition, 17
   errors, 79
   function scope, 77
   functional and physical agreement, 72
   independence, 18, 19, 22
   kick-off, 67
   need for conducting, 66
   objective, 65
   objective audit criteria, 65, 66, 67
   planning, 78
   plans, 66, 72, 84
   process applications, 69
   configuration audits, 72
      definition, 72
      functional and physical agreement, 72
      objective, 72
   functional configuration audit, 74
      activities, 74
      objective, 74
      report, 75
      testing scenerios, 74
   in-process audit, 71
      activities, 71
      objectives, 71
      for process execution consistency, 72
      for product consistency, 71
      report, 71
   involving the audited organization, 71
   physical configuration audit, 73
      activities, 73
      objective, 73
      report, 73
   prerequisites, 22
   process quality audit, 22
   product quality audit, 22
   quality program evaluation, 69
   quality systems audit, 22, 69
   Software Quality Program Audit, 69
      activities, 70
      objectives, 69
      report, 71
   process definition, 66
   recommendations, 67
   report, 69
   roles, 66
   sampling, 67
   SQPA executive summary, 87
   SQPA milestones, 84
   SQPA recommendations, 85
   SQPA results report, 85
   staff, 78, 79
   to verify in-process conformance, 9

Common software development problems, 92
Configuration management, critical activities, 10
Cost of quality, 1, 8
  maintenance costs, 13
  Quality/Cost curve, 13
  software error costs, 13
  technology-based cost issues, 15
Critical software, 56
Culture, 37
Customer, 17, 21, 58
  expectations, 13, 77, 87
  operations, 8
Customer and supplier involvement, 8

Development managers, 9, 33
Development process planning, 59
Documentation, 7
  customer-deliverable, 3, 92
  design specifications, 3, 20, 51
  development plan, 3, 51
  hierarchy of integrated planning documents, 51
  in-process, 92
  the plan as a product, 51
  project plan, 51
  reports, 3
  requirements specifications, 3, 6, 8
  Software Verification and Validation Plan, 55
  software verification diagrams, 9
  standards, 4, 59, 91
  standards taxonomy, 91
  test effort, 3, 20

Feasibility studies, 37
Firmware, 3, 7

Hardware, 7

In-process auditing, 61, 63
Inspection used in manufacturing, 21
Interviewing, 82
  active listening, 83
  elements of success, 82
  preparation, 82
  questioning, 76, 83
  skill improvement, 83

Maintenance, 7
  adaptive, 7
  corrective, 7
  perfective, 7
Management review, 24
  initiation, 25
  need for conducting, 25
  process definition, 25
  report, 26
  roles, 25
  statement of objectives, 24, 25
Market analysis, 37

Organizational design, 8

Process:
  control, 7, 9
    activities, 9
    components, 9
    configuration management, 9, 10
    conflict, 9, 10
    conflict diagram, 11
    interdependency, 11
    objectives, 9, 24, 33
    over-specification, 4
    project management, 9, 10
    quality management, 9, 10
    relative maturity of controls, 11
  definition, 2, 7, 8
  environment, 7, 12
    business, 13
    company, 12
    job, 12
    project, 12
    task, 12
Process technology, 13, 14, 93
  controlled process evolution, 13, 93
    award and reward, 94
    critical program steps, 93
    decision support, 95
      measurement opportunities, 96
      recommendations, 95
    as a journey, 93
    key elements, 93
    knowledge base maintenance, 94
    recommendations, 96
  controlling improvement, 15
  definition, 3
  improvement, 6, 24

improvement project:
  facilitator, 36
  leader, 16, 38
  managing feedback, 38
  managing the teams, 38
  milestones, 15, 30
  newsletter, 38
  project team, 16
  resource leader, 16
  secretary, 16
  special interest groups, 38
  steering committee, 15, 16
  supporting improvement, 17
improvement project review, 15, 16
  cause definition, 15, 31
  project sponsorship, 15, 30
  remedy identification and trial readiness, 15, 31
  remedy proven, 15, 32
  remedy transitioned, 15, 32
  reports, 16
macro-model definition, 7
maturity, 33
Product:
  definition, 3
  partitioning, 59
Product life, 14
Product review, 20
  acceptance and participation, 51, 58
  alternatives, 20
  attributes of successfull programs, 58
  data analysis, 61
  defect class, 63
  defect severity, 63
  defect type, 63
  discussion items list, 61
  execution consistency, 59
  execution support, 60
  feedback, 51, 61
  key inspection benefits, 21
  management responsibilities, 58
  meeting notice, 61
  process application planning, 50, 51, 52
    multiple examinations, 51, 56
    selection, 52, 53
  process definitions, 20, 21, 22
  process execution consistency, 50, 51
  process uniqueness, 50
  process variance, 63
  product checklist, 61
  to reduce large-project costs, 20
  repeatability, 50
  review entry checklist, 61
  review report form, 61
  rework report form, 61
  role descriptions, 61
  technical staff responsibilities, 58
  widely known applications, 51
Product technology, 13, 93
  definition, 3
  product realization, 6, 24
  product realization project:
    milestones, 20, 26
    project reviews, 19
  product realization project review:
    concept closure, 20, 27, 52
    decision-making authority, 19
    general market availability, 20, 29
    product maturity, 20, 29
    product realization, 20, 28
    product retirement, 20, 29
    project definition, 20, 27, 52
    trial readiness, 20, 28
Program:
  controls, 4
  definition, 3
Program source code, 3
Project:
  definition, 2
  two distinct categories, 6, 23
Project management, critical activities, 10
Project review, 33
  acceptance and participation, 33
  authority, 35
    business decision, 36
    managerial prerogative, 36
  controlling the mix, 36
  dress rehearsals, 34
  execution consistency, 34, 35
  feedback, 37
  key challenges, 33
  management education, 35
  management exposure and response, 35
  policy statement, 35, 36, 38
  reliance on project planning, 35
  reliance on standards, 35
  stage fright, 33, 34
  standard meeting protocol, 33, 35
    agenda, 33
    discussing blame, 33

Project review, (cont.)
    ownership, 33, 36
    results reporting, 36
    success criteria, 37

Quality management, 88
    activities, 88, 90
    roles, 88
    software quality assurance, 90
    software quality control, 91

Report writing, 84, 88
    literary suicide, 87
Required reviewer matrix, 59
Review:
    definition, 17
    managerial (or project) review, 17
    technical (or product) review, 17
Review and audit:
    activity perspectives, 6
    commonalities, 18
    controlled application, 6
    distinctions between, 17, 18
Review packet, 60

Software element, 72
    definition, 3
Software inspection, 44
    checklist, 47
    defect list, 47
    distinction, 44, 46
    exit decision, 47
    initiation, 46
    meeting agenda, 47
    misdirected reward, 95
    need for conducting, 46
    objective, 44
    process definition, 46
    product disposition distributions, 95
    reading:
        line-by-line, 45
        by paraphrasing, 45
    reports, 48
    rework verification, 47
    roles, 45
    statement of objectives, 44
    synergy, 45
    training, 45

Statement of objectives:
    cause definition review, 31
    concept closure review, 27
    general market availability review, 29
    product maturity review, 29
    product realization review, 28
    product retirement review, 30
    project definition review, 27
    project sponsorship review, 30
    remedy identification and trial readiness, review, 32
    remedy proven review, 32
    remedy transitioned review, 32
    software inspection, 44
    technical review, 42
    trial readiness review, 28
    walkthrough, 48

Technical review, 41
    initiation, 42
    need for conducting, 42
    objective, 41
    process definition, 43
    report, 44
    roles, 42
    statement of objectives, 42

Validation, 8
    definition, 3
    of process, 8
    of product, 8
Verification, 8
    definition, 3
    of process, 8
    of product, 8
Verification and validation:
    activities, 9
    objectives, 8
    plans, 3, 9, 55

Walkthrough, 48
    distinction, 48, 49
    initiation, 49
    need for conducting, 49
    objective, 48
    process definition, 49
    report, 50
    roles, 49
    statement of objectives, 48
Work breakdown structure, 37